FLY WITH NO FEAR

STOP FLYING WITH PHOBIA! END PANIC, ANXIETY, CLAUSTROPHOBIA AND FEAR OF FLYING FOREVER! OVERCOME YOUR ANTICIPATORY ANXIETY AND DEVELOP SKILLS TO HAVE A CONFIDENT & RELAXED FLYING

WRITTEN BY

RYAN TRIP

Contents

It's a common thing to find in the hearts of many, the fear of flying; as its mostly attached to the fear of heights. In this book titled '**FLY WITH NO FEAR**' with the subtitle '*STOP FLYING WITH PHOBIA! END PANIC, ANXIETY, CLAUSTROPHOBIA AND FEAR OF FLYING FOREVER! OVERCOME YOUR ANTICIPATORY ANXIETY AND DEVELOP SKILLS TO HAVE A CONFIDENT & RELAXED FLYING*', teaches you the steps to get rid of that flying fear.

You will learn and understand, why and how flying is the safest means of movement? and why flying by air is so important?!

This Document aims to provide precise and reliable details on this subject and the problem under discussion.

The product is marketed on the assumption that no officially approved bookkeeping or publishing house provides other available funds.

Where a legal or qualified guide is required, a person must have the right to participate in the field.

A statement of principle, which is a subcommittee of the American Bar Association, a committee of publishers and Associations and approved. A copy, reproduction, or distribution of parts of this text, in electronic or written form, is not permitted.

The recording of this Document is strictly prohibited, and any retention of this text is only with the written permission of the publisher and all Liberties authorized.

The information provided here is correct and reliable, as any lack of attention or other means resulting from the misuse or use of the procedures, procedures, or instructions contained therein is the total and absolute obligation of the user addressed.

The author is not obliged, directly or indirectly, to assume civil or civil liability for any restoration, damage, or loss resulting from the data collected here. The respective authors retain all copyrights not kept by the publisher.

The information contained herein is solely and universally available for information purposes. The data is presented without a warranty or promise of any kind.

The trademarks used are without approval, and the patent is issued without the trademark owner's permission or protection.

The logos and labels in this book are the property of the owners themselves and are not associated with this text.

Do you want to travel to inland areas and watch the globe -- with no panic attacks? You might have aviophobia, or even the anxiety about flying, then you can find means by which you may keep it from adversely impacting your lifetime. Currently being knowledgeable, with relaxation methods and preparation that your excursion are typical ways by which you may overcome your anxiety and also be liberated to learn more about the whole world. This is one undeniable fact which may find you moving: the chances of a plane crashing is 1 in 11 million. There is a whopping 0.00001percent possibility that anything could go horribly wrong during a flight.

Arming yourself with compliments concerning Air Planes

1.   Understand how secure planes are everywhere. Understanding that a statistic may possibly be unable to wholly help save you when your airplane leaves the runway. However, while you observe that traveling within a plane is very safe and sound, you're able to let yourself feel comfortable about your own trip in addition to your own way into the airport terminal. Even the truth of the topic is the fact that traveling is indeed safe and sound. Definitely, it is the most powerful manner of transport.

When traveling into a developed nation, your opportunities dying in a plane crash will be just one in thirty million.

2.   Examine the Security of airplane traveling along with Different hazards." There are plenty of different adventures in living you probably never ever think hard about. It works out they truly are more threatening than traveling in a plane. These threats are not intended to force you to truly feel stressed concerning these. As an alternative, they truly are intended to explain to you the way your problems concerning flying are! Know such numbers, compose them down, and also replicate them when you begin to be concerned about what's going to happen on the next trip.

>>> Your probability to be involved in a car crash are just 1 in 5,000. This usually means that probably the hardest part of one's airport trip is the driveway into the airport terminal. When you have left the driveway into the airport, then tap on your backside.

You have only managed to get through the very damaging facet of the trip.

>>> You've got a high possibility of dying of food poisoning compared to at a plane accident, in 13 million.

Additionally, you possess an increased likelihood of being afflicted by a snake bite, getting struck by electric shock, spilling of hot water or even falling from your mattress. In the event you are left, it really is more straightforward to use pre-assembled gear than it will perish in a plane accident.

You might be more inclined to experience falling while walking in the airplane.

3. Anticipate moves and senses throughout your trip. A big thing to be fearful of is maybe not knowing what's going to happen later. Why your airplane is moving

really rapidly? Why would my ears feel funny? Exactly why can the wing appear odd? Exactly why are we getting requested to continue to keep our seat straps? When posed using an odd circumstance, your very first instinct will be always to assume the worst. To do so, discover all you can about traveling and also the way a plane works. The further you realize, the less probability there'll soon be that you are worried about. Below are a few things which you ought to understand:

>>> The airplane should accomplish abound of speed in order for it to take off. This is exactly the reason you might feel as if the airplane is moving very rapidly. The moment the aircraft lifts off the bottom, you won't see the air craft's speed to be that much.

>>> Your ears are affected when the airplane goes down or up due to a big change in atmospheric pressure.

Particular regions of the wing are all assumed to maneuver throughout the trip. That is absolutely normal. These command surfaces have been made to drive atmosphere whereas the craft moves, so permitting the craft to be more light in the air.

4. Know just what things to anticipate with turbulence. Turbulence takes place every time a plane flies as a result of a place of reduced pressure to a high strain that is likely to force you to be feeling a "bulge" during your trip. Turbulence is the same as driving a rugged highway. It cannot induce the airplane to stall and begin falling out of the skies.

Around in some infrequent situations, turbulence induces harms, it is often due to the fact that travelers were not wearing seat straps and were injured by decreasing overhead bags. Consider it, you never have heard about the pilot hurt when there's turbulence. That is due to the fact that pilots wear seat straps.

5.   Find out more about the way the plane functions. You might also understand the inner workings of the plane to demystify the procedure that's in you. Studies reveal that 73 percent of men and women who're scared of combating anxiety have mechanical issues that may happen throughout a trip. But the further you realize about the way the plane operates, the longer in ease you are going to be through the duration of the procedure.

>>> Four forces have been on the job to have the airplane to fly: All these forces are equally balanced to let your flight really feel as easy and natural as strolling. Just as just one pilot claimed, "Planes would be the speediest in the atmosphere " You may research around the science supporting those compels in the event that you'd like to have your comprehension for the following degree.

>>> Jet engines are a lot more easily compared to engines you are going to see in an automobile or maybe at a lawnmower. At an unlikely event that anything goes wrong with a few of those airplane engines, the airplane is going to work just great having its own redundant engines.

6.   Simply believed, the airplane door will not open throughout flight. You must also

suppress any anxiety you might feel during your trip. The doorways have been intended to close first therefore the cabin stress (on average more compared to 1-1 psi) must be overcome until the doors might be dropped open. The moment you hit 30,000 feet (9,144.0 m), then there'll soon be approximately 20,000 lbs of tension retaining the door closed.

7.   Understand that planes are maintained often. Airplanes proceed via a whole lot of maintenance and repair techniques. For each hour a plane flies in the atmosphere, it had gone through 1 hour of care. It follows that in case your trip has been just three hours, the airplane goes through 3 hrs of care to be certain everything is functioning effortlessly!

Managing Your Anxiety

1.	Control your general anxiety.

You'll be able to really go a considerable way in controlling your nervousness about flying by becoming mindful about managing your anxiety generally. First, recognize your stress. Just how does one begin to truly feel anxious? Do your palms sweat? Do your palms tingle? By knowing exactly what signs you feel first, you will be able to begin handling exercises earlier to control your feelings of anxiety.

2.	Let go of everything you cannot control.

A lot of people who are scared of flying are fearful because they believe they aren't in control. People with this phobia might feel as if they are going to not ever get into a car wreck because they are driving. They are on the driver's seat. This can be the reason why they could accept the possibility of driving an automobile. Somebody else is still driving, up from the sky, so the absence of you as the controller is often one of the strangest things about flying.

A lot of men and women experience anxiety because of perceived management (or lack thereof) within a stressful circumstance.

3.   Strive Calming exercises to relieve nervousness.

Integrate anxiety-reducing exercises into your everyday life. Whenever you exercise, whenever you're perhaps not worried, you'll have equipment that will allow you to calm down when you could be worried. Then you definitely will really feel more competent to obtain control and calm yourself. Try yoga or meditation to cut back anxiety in your own life.

It is crucial to remember that your anxiety and nervousness might take a couple weeks to conquer and attain complete control.

4.   Strive to relax your muscles.

Begin with discovering what muscular band is equally rigid or tight. Shoulders are an excellent illustration. Usually, if we are stressed, we take our shoulders up and then tighten those muscles.

Have a deep breath and then let the shoulders sink. Have the muscles relax. Now try that with other muscle groups like your face or your own legs.

5.   Use directed imagery.

Think of an area that makes you happy or comfortable. Imagine you're in that place.

What do you see? Scent? Feel? Focus on each detail in regards to the spot you pick.

You can find several guided vision tapes that you may acquire or even download to help you practice.

6.   Simply take deep breaths.

Put one hand on your tummy. Just breathe deeply with your nose again. Take in all of the atmospheres you are able to. You need to feel your belly rise, maybe not your torso. Exhale through your mouth. Agree with your abdomen to push out all of the atmospheres.

Do so 4-5 times to help you flake out.

Remember that breathing workout routines may perhaps not provide adequate relief. Several recent research studies found no quantifiable advantage.

7.   Distract yourself.

Consider something else you're excited about or at least something which will take your mind from your own fears. What can you make for supper? In the event that you could move anywhere, where do you proceed? What will you really do?

8.   You require a Class.

There are classes that can assist you to overcome the fear of traveling. You might want to pay for one of these lessons, however, they really do exist. Now, there are two sorts of courses: people who attend and people who really do at their own pace with MP4 videos, published stuff and counseling periods. Groups you show up at enabling you to get accustomed to flying, exposure to an airport and also a trip by means of your class leader. The desensitization obtained by accepting this flight might never survive, but if you don't retain it by traveling usually.

You'll be able to explore such category treatment classes in your region.

Classes done at your own pace render you in charge of the practice. And, since you retain the course stuff, you're able to reinforce your understanding through the substances occasionally.

Some classes provide weekly group phone counseling sessions at no additional cost.

Some classes set you in a flight simulator. This imitates the experience of traveling without even moving an inch.

9.   Simply take flying courses.

Deal with your fear head-on by taking flying lessons. You'll find countless tales of people who've feared something each of their lives only to meet it face to face a single day. Then they detect that the thing of their fear was nothing to be terrified of. One solution to overcome a phobia is to immerse yourself into what you understand can be really a safe situation. Within this circumstance, you're in the clear presence of a trained practitioner.

With the guidance of your instructor, you might find that traveling by air isn't so frightening after all. Though it's definitely an extreme strategy, it could become your means of relieving your own anxiety.

10.   Steer Clear of reading things related to plane crashes.

If you prefer to keep calm on the subject, don't worry about airplane crashes which can be recorded from the news. These testimonies aren't going to cause you to feel better. Instead, they are going to only add to your anxiety about an improbable event occurring. If you are struggling to overcome your stress about flying, avoid the desire to gratify your fears.

The same holds for seeing Flight or other pictures about aircraft crashes or flights that are frightening.

All of us, experience stresses every once in a while. In little doses, stress may be described as a great thing for the reason that it enables you to comprehend when matters are not perfect. But migraines may collect more than what's necessary and induce a lasting state of stress which starts retraining the mind. Emotions of concern and fear something awful can occur which can permeate day to day life, which makes it hard to unwind and relish the current minute. Sometimes stress goes down if its origin disappears off, however, for all persons that succeed, shooting out the joy of daily life. Taking time to create fresh physical and mental customs would be step one in becoming aided.

Relaxing the Body

1. Require deep breaths.

Pause that which you're undertaking and concentrate completely in your own breath. While you inhale, then draw on the atmosphere in your stomach, as opposed to only your upper torso. After that, exhale through your nose again. Continue this procedure five days, then restart breathing. Your torso needs to feel fuller, permitting one to simply take in deeper breaths.

You may ensure you're breathing profoundly by placing a hand in your tummy so you are able to sense it increase.

2. Take your own position.

The human body wants to guard itself once you are feeling stressed, however, also changing things indicates into the brain that you're in charge. Press back your shoulders and straighten your backbone, and then lift your own chin. You are going to begin to experience calmness and control over your anxiety.

3. Go for a stroll.

Strolling of the human body is able to alter you of the condition of stress. Not just does this take the head off what is triggering your own nervousness, but walking additionally releases endorphins which may help you in feeling much better. In the event that you are able to, select the walkout, investing some time in having a chat mate while strolling can even enhance your feeling.

Any undertaking which is able to assist you to proceed forward away from your own anxiety should be done.

4.   Can yoga do it?

An everyday yoga exercise is able to assist you to relax your stress and cut back the human body's reaction to tension. Enroll at a yoga course or take to an education video clip or publication.

As an instance, you might do 10 minutes of yoga in the daytime. In the event you exercise regularly, it will certainly be more painless to complete whenever you truly feel stressed and will need to unwind.

5.   Carry out innovative muscular comfort.

Beginning in your feet, tense and relax every single part of your own nerves. Once you perform on your own feet, proceed up for the next feet. Keep on till you get to the surface of your face. This ought to make you better.

You're far from alone if you're scared of flying. According to FlyFright, almost a third of Americans are either anxious about flying or scared to fly. Fortunately? You do not need to let these fears avoid you from pursuing your desire to study abroad or to take a trip to the world. Here are a few ways to conquer your worry of flying.

1. Fake it till you make it.

While the power of positive thinking will not keep your plane up, it will help keep you relaxed until you reach your location.

"There's a lot to be stated for fabricating confidence in any circumstance, however specifically when it worries battling stress, anxieties, and worries. You'll discover yourself to be much calmer if you behave like someone who does not have a fear of flying. Pretend that you're somebody who takes pleasure in flying and your brain will be able to sign up the reasoning that planes are the safest mode of transport which the possibilities of something catastrophic happening are minute."

2. Use your rational mind.

Practically speaking, flying is much better in terms of safety. In addition, airplane crashes are catastrophic, killing more individuals at once, which grabs more attention and makes people more sensitive to them.

One of the simplest methods to banish those runaway ideas and worries? For beginners, according to statistics shared by FlyFright, there's only an infinitesimal chance of being involved in an aircraft mishap.

3. Resolve your anxiety.

Anticipatory anxiety is how we are feeling in lieu of fear. It is often the most intense stress and anxiety you will experience throughout your flight, however, it is not an accurate predictor of how you will feel on the flight.

We have actually already covered one way to keep stress and anxiety at bay: informing yourself of the facts. Smile even if you do not feel like smiling. Relax your body and a lot of individuals will discover their emotions will follow when this is done.

4. Select your seat wisely.

Turbulence can be worrying to even the most skilled tourists, while a loud flight can even more intensify your tension. Picking a seat at the front of the plane can be a smoother flight. Plus, according to one JetBlue pilot, "There's less sound when you're sitting forward on the wings". In many airplanes, the engines lie under the wings. Sitting in the front of the wing is like being behind a speaker. All the sounds of the engine and the disturbed air are forecasted away from you."

Window seats produce a sense of location by being able to reference the ground, while aisle seats enable for euphoric lack of knowledge. Middle seats give you two armrests to grip."

While you're on your way to your seat (and before the aircraft is in the air), meanwhile, why not ask a flight attendant if you can make a stop at the cockpit? "Such sight is satisfying to individuals and creates flying trust, as does seeing a practical control panel."

5. Think about expert intervention.

These consist of professional counseling, medication, and hypnosis. There are even online courses readily available making up practical suggestions and actionable insights into coping with your fear of flying.

If you're afraid of flying, you're far from alone. According to FlyFright, nearly a 3rd of Americans are either distressed about flying or afraid to fly.

There are others that are exceptionally inconvenient to dodge, like flying. "Worry of flying is an acknowledged and categorized fear that affects millions of individuals throughout the world," says Alexia Touboul, LMHC, Clinical Director at Banyan Treatment.

In an effort to help those facing flying fears, we interviewed a host of experts who might speak about particular fear conquering, even when the specific worry is an issue. It does seem that as it relates to flights, many people are afraid of a 'worst-case scenario,' which may be different for everyone, and not necessarily logical," states Jamie Price, co-founder of the emotional wellness app Stop, Breathe & Think that suggests brief customized meditations and activities for particular emotions. "For me, it's about the aircraft being pirated. It could be about falling for others. It may be as basic as fretting about missing out on the flight, or sensation worried about going through security. The common thread here is our response to tension and strong feelings like worry, which starts in the brain." Here are some strategies we learned that are here to help.

Get a weighted blanket

Weighted blankets have actually been sold online for about twenty years, mainly targeted to people on the autism spectrum, however, they're having a moment in the tension- and sleep-related market. A weighted blanket soothes by motivating your body to release serotonin and dopamine through deep pressure touch; you'll know how amazing this feels if you've ever felt at ease while getting dental X-rays were done. "When you have actually prepared with therapy and are ready to get on your flight, smaller sized weighted products like a weighted lap pad or weighted shoulder wrap can be valuable along with some soothing sound in your headphones, and perhaps even an eye mask," Chambers states.

Practice makes perfect

When it worries enlisting the help of a certified professional, you'll have great deals of treatment choices to try depending upon who you deal with. "A radical, but reliable, a technique to treatment is Direct exposure Therapy, where patients take part in simulations meant to mirror the experience of flying under the supervision and guidance of a therapist. Your therapist helps recondition your actions to flying, trying to take it from a hellish to safe experience. If you have a wedding event to fly to this weekend, Exposure Therapy won't be the answer to your prayers. "This kind of work requires time as it resembles exercising in the health club, you can't expect the abs overnight," states Dr. Kate Cummins, a certified scientific psychologist who focuses on neuropsychology, health psychology, and travel assessment," hence this type of cognitive work takes some time and practice as well as direct exposure to flights in order to acknowledge that the majority of the time, flying is a non-traumatic action."

Reprogram your brain

You can feel rumbles in your tummy, pounding in your heart and faster beats, or straining in your muscles. The secret is to discover how to take yourself out of this stressful loop, and there are a couple of mindful workouts that can assist you to do that. When you observe that your mind has roamed to your worries, simply label it 'thinking' and then gently bring your attention back to your breath going in and out."

Avoid phony news with real intel

"Oftentimes, a worry response is triggered by an emotional reaction in the battle or flight the mechanism, so providing accurate knowledge and mindfulness workouts can decrease the initial response attached to stress and anxiety and fear," Cummins says.

"While this was a hugely tragic event, it did highlight deficiencies in global airport security, and because then huge improvements have actually been made," Sage-Passant states. The United States Aviation Administration has found out that there's only a very low chance of air mishaps and you have a 96% possibility of surviving a mishap," states Sage-Passant.

Keep breathing

As someone who had PTSD issues, I had crazy stress and anxiety and claustrophobia that made flying extremely tough," says Anthony Treas, Miles Per Hour, a men's health and brain performance coach. "My favourite is the 5-3-5 respiration method; inhale for Five seconds, retain for three seconds, exhale for Five seconds and replicate up until feeling calmer," states

Touboul. If your creativity is failing you, swipe through said images on your phone.

Treat your whole self

When you get frightened, there is a lot of crap that goes down. With numerous layers of bad taking place simultaneously, many layers of treatment may be essential. For example, a certified psychological health counselor, Alex Runolfson, who owns and operates Flower Recovery, a practice that focuses on trauma and anxiety disorders concentrates on dealing with the entire person rather than only dealing with specific elements of stress and anxiety. I start with teaching them various relaxation techniques consisting of progressive muscle relaxation, breathing exercises, and different container exercises; this helps them not just stay calm and collected during treatment however likewise provides that sense of control that they thought was missing out on," Runolfson states. "I then help customers recognize particular triggers consisting of the worst part of flying (i.e. turbulence, the sound of the engines, the vibration, the odor, and so on), specific limiting beliefs (i.e 'I'm not in control.'), emotions (i.e worry, stress and anxiety, embarrassment, and so on), and body experiences (i.e. racing heart, tight stomach, muscle stress, difficulty breathing, etc.). I then present bilateral stimulation (having their eyes return and forth or gentle tapping on alternating knees) and help them proceed in between what they rationally know and what they mentally feel." The treatment is developed to "reboot" your brain to air flying without having a panic action.

It seems once it applies to flying, the majority of individuals are scared of a 'worst-case circumstance,' which may be in variations for everyone, and not necessarily rational. An efficient, method to ease the situation as stated earlier in this book is the Exposure Therapy, where individuals are made take part in simulations indicated to mirror the experience of flying under the guidance and guidance of a therapist; says Touboul. This sort of activity takes a long period, as it's comparable to working out in the fitness center, you can't anticipate perfection overnight," says Dr. Kate Cummins, a licensed scientific psychologist who specializes in neuropsychology, health psychology, and travel consultation, "thus this type of cognitive work takes time and practice as well as direct exposure to flights in order to acknowledge that many of the time, flying is a non-traumatic occasion."

1.	Latch on to the stimuli that put you up.

Find out what frightens you and analyze how your anxiety reaction is activated. Your goal is to determine your particular triggers, so you can handle your worry when stress and anxiety rates are small. Knowing what starts you off will make it a lot easier to shut it off.

2.	Move over to the plane with understanding.

Stress and anxiety thrives on ignorance and feeds off "what if?" disastrous thoughts. When you end up being well-informed, your "what if?" ideas are limited by the facts. End up being familiar with the realities. They will not eliminate your anxiety, however, they will help you handle it.

3.   Expect your stress and anxiety.

Anticipatory stress and anxiety are what we experience in anticipation of fear. It is frequently the most intense stress and anxiety you will experience during your flight, however, it is not a precise predictor of how you will feel on the flight. It is often far greater than what you in fact experience.

4.   A Separate worry from risk.

It is often hard to separate anxiety from danger due to the fact that your body reacts in precisely the same way to both. Tell yourself that anxiety lets your negative thinking feel very likely to take place, and advise yourself that feeling anxious doesn't imply you are in danger.

5.   Acknowledge these points

Part A: Anxiety tricks common sense.

Anxiety will fool you into believing you remain in danger when you are perfectly safe. Your gut feelings in these circumstances will constantly tell you to stay clear, however, if you follow these sensations, you will always be reinforcing your anxiety.

Part B: You can outmaneuver anxiety.

As a rule, do the reverse of what distressed sensations are telling you to do. Fight what the stress and anxiety is telling you to do, but embrace the pain that stress and anxiety bring.

6.   Move on over when bumps happen while flying.

To manage stress and anxiety when turbulence strikes, learn about airplanes and how they are developed to manage turbulence. Focus on managing your stress and anxiety, rather than when the turbulence will end or how serious it may get. Remind yourself that you are safe.

7.   Educate fellow fly mates on how to help you.

Other fly mates need to understand what terrifies you, along with what helps you most to cope with anxiety throughout a flight. Your job is to be clear about your triggers and ask Particularly because of what you deem really useful.

8.   Value each flying moment

Exposure is the main thing to conquer the anxiety. Every flight provides you with the chance to make the next one simpler. Your aim is to reskill your brain to get less sensitive to the stimuli that starts you off.

Figure out what terrifies you and take a look at how your anxiety reaction is set off. Your objective is to determine your specific triggers, so you can handle your fear when anxiety levels are low. It's also the most powerful anxiety you're going to feel. throughout your flight, however, it is not a precise predictor of how you will feel on the flight. It is frequently hard to separate anxiety from risk due to the fact that your body responds in exactly the very same method to both. Tell yourself that stress and anxiety make your frightening ideas feel more likely to occur, and advise yourself that feeling anxious doesn't imply you are in danger.

Other Strategies:

1.   Consider the Number

Catastrophic ideas constantly originate from a "what if" mindset. However, statistically speaking, the possibilities of getting harmed in an airplane are less than getting hit by lightning. Driving a vehicle is 100 times more fatal than flying, and traveling by motorcycle is 3,000 times more of a threat. In reality, as per the Global Air Transport AuthoritySecurity Report a few years ago, there was only one significant accident for each 5.4 million flights. So, you're in fact much safer in the sky than on the road.

2.   Take efforts against the fear

Many airline companies and airports use courses for those who have fear. Among the best ones are the Concern of Flying Clinic at the San Francisco International Airport Terminal (SFO), which makes use of cognitive behavior modification. Furthermore, British Airways has a Flying With Positive self-image course, EasyJet has a Courageous Flyer program, and also Virgin Atlantic has a Traveling Without Anxiety workshop. These sessions are led by pilots, airline company assistants, as well as psychotherapists to educate vacationers, passengers, tourists, etc. on exactly how to overcome their anxieties.

3.   Select Your Position Sensibly

In some cases the tiniest modifications can keep you relaxed. Be tactical about where you wish to rest on the airplane: seats in front have less turbulence and aisles have more space and permit you to get up and move around if you feel worried (plus, they're farther from the windows if you have a worry of heights). We'd likewise advise spending lavishly on an upgrade to first class-- after all, a little free drink and motion pictures never ever harm-- and on an overnight flight, you can recline into a comfortable bed and snuggle up to capture some sleep.

4.   Download Anti-Anxiety Apps.

VALK-- a pseudo-in-flight therapist-- is another favorite as it displays flight safety data as well as weather and wind projections. There's also a panic button that triggers immediate stress-management suggestions and techniques.

5.   Learn basics about Flying a planes

A lot of individuals have a fear of flying since they do not understand how planes work. For people who find out best by doing, sign up for a discovery flight on a small craft with a personal pilot who can inform you of some of the scarier aspects of the sky.

6.   Load Diversions.

This may seem cliche, however, it's always wise to bring activities on an aircraft. It makes the whole process go quicker, and it sets your attention on something aside from the flight. Ensure to download your preferred movies, TV podcasts, shows, or playlists. You can likewise throw in the season's best book, that stack of nightstand magazines you've been suggesting to get to, or a coloring adult book (which has been shown to relieve the mind). Lengthy-haul flights are always a perfect time to deal with some self-care:

bring a sheet mask and a silk eye mask for an appeal rest. For individuals who find out best by doing, sign up for a discovery flight on a little craft with a personal pilot who can inform you of some of the scarier elements of the sky.

If you are like most people looking for solutions, there is a likelihood you are hoping you can check out a hypnotherapist for one session and your flying worries will amazingly go away.

If only this is held true. For the huge majority of individuals, fears, like most anxiety worries, take some time to work through and aren't ameliorated throughout a workplace visit.

That's not to state it does not occur for some people. But, as per the research report, here's the great news. When hypnotherapy is being used to make it easier for other kinds of anxiety treatment, such as CBT, people tend to have significant results.

What is essential that you know is this. Hypnosis isn't a "treatment" in itself. Rather, It is an item that can be counted upon to assist in other types of treatment.

Can hypnosis assist me in flying?

Fear of Flying Hypnotherapy-- Common Bond

Many individuals who wonder about using hypnotherapy for flying worries normally share numerous typical characteristics. Can you relate to any of these?

Prior disappointment flying (Awful instability) has raised stress levels. A Challenge giving up authority to someone.

You might be wondering how hypnotherapy works for stress and anxiety, panic, and phobias?

Assuming you are dealing with somebody who is a licensed psychological health specialist who likewise holds board accreditation in medical hypnotherapy, the following typically occurs:

Typical activities;

An initial consultation to discuss your worry of flying that includes an evaluation of your individual health history (medical, mental health, etc.). A potential recommendation to your doctor to dismiss medical causes for stress and anxiety, such as a physical condition or medications that might be triggering you to experience worry, fear, and tension for determination if hypnotherapy as part of psychotherapy is appropriate for your situation.

Cognitive practice sessions through guided imagery, which is an essential of hypnotherapy.

An evaluation of how your anxiety has actually been decreased through therapy utilizing Subjective Structures of

Distress(SUDS). Adjunct hypnotherapy intended to promote calmer reactions to flying while helping you to become desensitized to aviation-related noises, movements (turbulence) and sights. Instruction on deep breathing methods, utilized as coping mechanisms. Guidance on how to utilize self-hypnosis and meditation to promote calmness.

An essential function of hypnotherapy for a fear of flying is innovative visualization, coupled with assisted imagery. Using this approach, a hypnotherapist will psychologically assist you through numerous flying situations.

You are conscious of your worries in such a way however not always "afraid". Calm distance is developed in between the numerous things that amp you up when flying, such as:

>>> Abrupt, unforeseen noises

>>> Turbulence

>>> Changes in cabin pressure

>>> Flight deck announcements

>>> Common airplane & strange airplane noises

Hypnotherapy for Fears and Flying

When you work with a licensed expert who provides hypnotherapy as part of anxiety counseling, you gain the insight of a specialist who is able to help you through working you through your phobias utilizing a variety of healing methods.

Common methods might consist of:

>>> Traditional Cognitive Behavioral Therapy

>>> Insight-Oriented Counseling

>>> Behavior Modification

>>> Relaxation Techniques (Relaxation Hypnosis)

>>> Approval and Dedication Therapy

>>> Exposure therapy (example: checking out the airport).

Is Hypnotherapy against flying fear right for me?

If you were dealing with a fear of flight that genuinely caused you to miss out on things like business trips, household holidays or visits to friends/relatives, hypnotherapy might be a powerful tool that can be sought.

Remember, if you have a fear of flying, you may have a stress and anxiety disorder. This means it is essential that you deal with a therapist that has the requisite education and training to assist with these types of worries.

A preliminary consultation to discuss your worry of flying that includes an assessment of your individual health history (medical, psychological health, etc.). A possible recommendation to your doctor to rule out medical causes for anxiety, such as a physical condition or medications that might be causing you to experience fear, worry, and tension for the determination if hypnotherapy as part of psychiatric therapy is appropriate for your situation.

There are many different causes of why someone would develop aerophobia. For example, it is not implausible to think that you may have been genetically predisposed to develop agoraphobia due to your ancestor's fear of heights.

Other factors regarding why somebody might establish aerophobia is that they themselves are survivors of a traumatizing airplane crash or possibly they know someone who lost his life in a plane crash. Besides being afraid of an airplane crashing, there is likewise the fear of the plane being pirated. Though the chances of being on a plane that was pirated by terrorists are roughly 1 in 10,408,947, it is still a prominent worry among those residing in numerous nations.

Another cause as to why someone may develop aerophobia is that unlike driving a boat or a car, you have absolutely no control of the plane. Even though planes maybe safer than cars statistically, the mere fact that people are unable to control or direct the plane in any capacity in the instance of an emergency leads many people to experience aerophobia.

Aerophobia Treatments.

There is no recognized treatment for this condition. Talk therapy and/or anti-anxiety medication may be able to help minimize symptoms. Talk treatment might be able to help reveal some of the underlying factors as to why their worry of aircraft is so extreme and out of touch with reality. Exposure therapy may be able to help treat aerophobia. This would be done by having the patient end up being slowly exposed to aircraft increasingly more in an effort to "desensitize" them from their fear of aircraft.

If you are uncertain regarding whether you have aerophobia or if you currently understand that you have it and you are wanting to get dealt with, then you need to talk to your physician as soon as you can so you can get appropriately dealt with. Your medical professional may ask that you see an expert such as a cognitive behavioral therapist, psychologist, or a psychiatrist to help treat your symptoms.

Treatments

Dialectical Behavior Therapy (DBT) for Aerophobia.

It is commonly used to deal with people suffering from a borderline personality disorder. These teams usually last for 6 months long and can start from two individuals to a number of individuals depending upon the number of people that join the team.

One extremely reliable DBT skill for assisting someone with agoraphobia is half-smiling. This strategy works by having you consider that which you fear or upsets you while slightly raising the corners of your mouth by gently smiling, hence the term "half-smiling." Although, it isn't adequate to simply think of your fear while half-smiling, you also need to refrain and try from amusing those uncomfortable emotions that your particular worry may evolve.

Mindfulness is also commonly employed in DBT and can considerably benefit someone with aerophobia as it is carried out in a group setting, which helps to put the client out of their convenience zone. These group mindfulness practices might consist of drinking warm tea to hone in on the sense of taste and tactile senses or simply concentrating on the breath.

Coping ahead is another very beneficial DBT skill that can assist someone with aerophobia. With managing ahead, you would need to find a location where you can take a seat silently without interruption. Close your eyes and then think of the many various possible circumstances where you would face your particular worry and overcome it or deal with it. Once you are finally exposed in reality to the common fear connected with it, doing so will help you to be much better adept at coping with your aerophobia.

Yoga for Aerophobia

There's a whole variety of different yoga positions that can be used to considerably benefit somebody who is suffering from aerophobia. In part, this is because of the meditative frame of mind that yoga tends to produce in those who practice it on a consistent basis. Yoga can be considered meditation in motion. It can help to ease a few of the stress and anxiety associated with aerophobia due to the simple reality that by taking part in yoga, your attention will be redirected to something more efficient.

There are several kinds of yoga that someone with aerophobia can gain from, such as hatha yoga or hot yoga, amongst lots of others. Regardless of the many different kinds of yoga that exist, virtually every one of them can assist to soothe some of the tension and stress and anxiety that is associated with aerophobia

It maybe in your benefit to take a class or view some guided video clips that can aid you through each situation if you have actually never ever practiced yoga before. Similar to meditation, the much more you practice yoga exercise, the extra skilled you will certainly come to be at it. Besides aiding you to reduce your signs and symptoms of aerophobia, you can also expect to acquire increased strength and flexibility, among other benefits.

Cognitive Behavioral Therapy (CBT) for Aerophobia.

CBT is a psycho-social treatment that aims to improve one's psychological wellness. It is a method that is commonly made use of to deal with individuals suffering from stress and anxiety conditions such as generalized stress and anxiety condition and OCD. Someone with aerophobia might additionally be able to benefit from CBT to viewing as how it would permit them to have a much better understanding regarding what they believe and also employ the method they carry out in relation to their irrational worries.

CBT could be totally helpful for one with aerophobia given the sheer automaticity of their symptoms. As an example, when somebody with aerophobia is revealed to their worry, they will generally have a rapid subconscious reaction to their concern. Such a lack of self-questioning is likely a huge part of why a person with this condition will certainly endure to the degree that they will. CBT can aid you to take a step back and also assess your anxieties much more deeply than you typically would.

Discovering to be more meticulous with regards to comprehending one's particular anxieties, someone with aerophobia engaging in CBT can also expect to learn various other skills aimed at helping to relieve the anxiety caused by their condition.

Mindfulness-Based Stress Reduction (MBSR) for Aerophobia.

MBSR is an 8-week evidence-based program that offers secular, extensive mindfulness training to assist people that are dealing with stress and anxiety, depression and fear, and also various other sorts of mental anguish. MBSR may be able to considerably assist a person who is suffering from acrophobia as mindfulness meditation has been shown to be very beneficial for anxious people. In such a structured program, a person with aerophobia can anticipate discovering a huge selection of various abilities that can help them to soothe the extreme anxiousness that's related to their particular anxiety.

Speak to your medical professional or specialist to see if MBSR can assist you to minimize the strength of your signs and symptoms of aerophobia, as well as where to find MBSR programs in your area.

Exposure Therapy for Aerophobia.

As formerly pointed out, exposure treatment is among the most usual methods to treat anxiousness disorders such as aerophobia. If the specialist were to somewhat reveal someone with acrophobia to their concern, then it might not be extremely effective as they might require a greater quantity of exposure to absolutely activate any type of beneficial change in the patient.

The very same can be claimed for the antithesis of this scenario. If the therapist were to exceedingly subject a person with acrophobia to their fear, then doing so could be highly counterproductive to the point to where their aerophobia may become immensely worse due to the therapy alone. It is important that an exposure therapy specialist performs on someone with aerophobia has a very strong sense of just how severe their symptoms are so that they can know the level of the exposure that the patient will likely be able to handle.

Reducing Caffeine for Aerophobia.

It is obvious that taking in huge amounts of caffeine throughout the day can aid in making you extra anxious. Such a mindset is usually a precursor for a person with aerophobia to experience panic attacks.

So, taking in little or no caffeine throughout the day might be able to significantly help reduce your day to day stress and anxiety. Although doing so will likely not make every one of your anxiety vanish, it will certainly undoubtedly help you to lower any unneeded suffering that you would certainly have or experienced if you were to consume a big amount of high levels of caffeine.

Beverages like coffee and also tea are commonly high in caffeine, as well as some power drinks. Actually, some foods have caffeine in them also, such as dark delicious chocolate. Being extra mindful of your daily caffeine intake might assist you to reduce a few of the signs associated with aerophobia.

Psychiatric Drugs for Aerophobia.
Antidepressant Drugs.

These kinds of drugs aren't just for individuals that suffer from anxiety as they can additionally help individuals experiencing stress and anxiety problems as well, such as aerophobia. Some typical antidepressants are Paxil, Zoloft, as well as Lexapro, among numerous others. These medicines might have the ability to help in reducing a few of the symptoms of aerophobia.

These kinds of medicines are typically handled on an everyday basis. They can indeed help avoid anxiety attacks from taking place, however, they are a lot more utilized to help reduce people's daily stress and anxiety. Speak with your doctor to see if taking antidepressants can assist in minimizing your signs and symptoms of aerophobia, along with whether it is safe to do so.

Anti-anxiety Medicines.

These sorts of medications are really useful to aid avoid panic attacks. Such drugs can be extremely valuable for individuals struggling with extreme agoraphobia as a result of the reality that people with phobias typically experience panic attacks as well. Some usual anti-anxiety medicines consist of Xanax, Valium, and Klonopin, amongst lots of others.

These types of medications are not commonly taken on a daily basis, however, they might be taken insofar as the individual's aerophobia is extreme enough. Nonetheless, this is something that you need to initially review with your doctor prior to you choosing to do so to guarantee that it works and you're secure.

Workout for Aerophobia.

Workout has been revealed to be exceptionally helpful for individuals suffering from anxiousness problems, including aerophobia. Particularly, a cardiovascular workout can significantly aid to alleviate one's anxiety. This is not to say that weight-resistance training would not benefit someone with anxiety, however, rather than that cardiovascular workout has been shown to be much more efficient at soothing those excellent chemicals in the brain, such as endorphins.

According to the American Psychology Association, the workout can help to task the mind to far better handle demanding situations. When we think about the high amount of tension that the body is put under during difficult exercise, this makes good sense. If you are inactive, then taking part in some form of cardiovascular exercise may have the ability to significantly help in reducing your signs of aerophobia by making it much easier for you to manage the anxiousness and also anxiety that's related to this condition.

There are various cardio techniques that you can partake in to help in reducing your symptoms of aerophobia, such as swimming, biking, snowboarding, walking, and running. You can additionally acquire many benefits of the workout by playing sports such as tennis, racquetball, soccer, and also basketball, among numerous other sports. Taking part in some form of exercise constantly may be able to help relieve a few of the discomfort associated with aerophobia gradually.

Meditation/Reflection for Aerophobia.

There are various types of meditation that exist which can be extremely helpful for someone struggling with aerophobia. Particularly, mindfulness meditation has actually been shown to be fairly beneficial for aiding individuals to participate in a more equanimous state. There are many different methods with which you can apply mindfulness reflection and also there are additionally various meditation applications that are made to make points as very easy as possible for you.

Mindfulness has the possibility to considerably assist those experiencing acrophobia because of how it will aid one to distract themselves from their anxiety by redoubling their focus onto another thing that does not have any kind of emotional luggage connected to it, such as by concentrating on the breath for example. This is just one of one of the most standard manner in which one can practice meditation and succeed.

For someone with aerophobia in the midst of an anxiety attack, rerouting one's focus to the various experiences felt when breathing can in fact aid to lower the quantity of psychological misery experienced during such an increase in anxiety.

To execute mindfulness meditation to aid relieve one's symptoms of aerophobia, you can do so by paying very close attention to the method the muscles in your abdominal area and also upper body agreement as well as unwind with every inhale and every breathing out. You can spend time dwelling on how it really feels as your upper body increases throughout each inhale and how it sinks in with every exhale.

Concentrating on your breathing, you can additionally focus on the sounds around you, the means your skin really feels as you touch specific objects, the way foods taste, in addition to how certain fragrances to scent. Basically, developing into your five sense organs can dramatically help you to lower the anxiousness that is related to aerophobia.

One extremely efficient DBT ability for assisting someone with agoraphobia is half-smiling. Coping ahead is another really beneficial DBT ability that can assist someone with aerophobia.

MBSR may well be able to offer substantial assistance to anyone suffering from acrophobia as mindfulness meditation has been shown to be very beneficial for anxious people. In such a structured program, someone with aerophobia can expect to learn a plethora of different skills that can help them to relieve the intense the anxiety that's associated with their specific phobia.

If the specialist was expected to over-expose somebody with acrophobia to their fear, then doing so could be highly counterproductive to the point to where their aerophobia may become immensely worse due to the therapy alone.

WHY ARE PLANES SO NECESSARY IN OUR PRESENT WORLD?

The aircraft; no doubt one of many significant developments of the 20th century, if not perpetuity. Let's be honest, absolutely nothing has come that has actually revolutionized our globe the way aviation has. No doubt, the internet is a quite good development, it really did not reduce the globe as it did link it. Air travel truly made this world little, transforming traveling times from months to a fraction of a day. A question I've posed is how would the world look like if the airplanes would have never been developed? To answer this, we need to dive into the background and also the production of the plane, as well as its development throughout the past 112 years.

Airplanes has always been in the dreams and also the creativities of different people as long as history can inform. For ages, some thought that sticking plumes to their arms would certainly help them fly. Unfortunately, those that thought that fell short significantly. It wasn't up until rather just recently when guys took to the air in a craft made to float in the air. Lots of people think that the Wright bros invented the airplane. Currently, it is true that they were the initial people to accomplish heavier-than-air flight, (although there is an intriguing debate that a New Zealand pilot made a successful flight twice prior to Wright's several months in advance), however, they definitely were not the first to work on planes or aircraft generally.

Actually, a dozen or more inventors had already made trips in heavier-than-air crafts, however, these crafts had no engines, as well as a result served no useful objective for the advancement in aeronautics and heavier-than-air flight. Even then individuals had been flying in dirigibles as well as balloons for about 1000 years. The first recorded glider trip occurred in 1010 when an English monk leaped from a tower as well as moved 200 meters. He was hurt yet lived to tell the story, making this a remarkable step forward in air trips. Nonetheless, a risk-free, sustained, manned trip did not take place until the 18th century, when the Montgolfier bros made the first successful hot air balloon trip. Europe is recognized with most of the advancements in aviation in the pre-Wright age days, with numerous effective balloon and dirigible trips, as well as introducing the advancement of moving. Otto Lilienthal was one of these terrific leaders. He made many effective trips in his gliders, but tragically, died while flying.

The Wright brothers were a peculiar set of brothers. Born and also raised in Dayton, Ohio, they started a tiny bicycle store, and soon afterward became enthralled in air travel. They constructed kites, gliders, wind tunnels, as well as several numerous versions, all to aid their process of accomplishing powered heavier-than-air trips. On December 17th, 1903, they attained what no man had actually done prior to them: they raised a powered craft heavier-than-air off the earth in a controlled way, as well as returned back safely. After this, aeronautics moved. It took less than one decade for an airplane to break the 10,000-foot mark, and less than 30 for all metal airplanes to make their way right into the skies. It just took a blistering 69 years for the forthcoming inventors to go from a 120 ft flight to traveling the 238,900 miles to the moon. That is unbelievable. Nothing, aside from electronic devices (though partially to aviation) has progressed as well as expanded faster than any other invention in history.

Currently, what would life really look like if the aircraft never ever existed? A frightening question without a doubt, but one that begs to be asked. Well, first of all, points would certainly be very extremely sluggish. It would take hours to get to places that once took a matter of minutes, it would certainly take almost a week to make it across the nation, and making it to trans-Atlantic and also transpacific destinations around the world would take months. We would certainly still remain in the 1990s in regards to modern technology, because of the airplane, stronger as well as more advanced computer systems and software came to help aircraft fly much longer, farther, higher, extra precisely, and a lot more effectively. Additionally, great deals of individuals would be dead as a result of car mishaps and also other occurrences in remote places where assistance could not begotten. Helicopters are effective as well as reliable devices at moving the damaged, swiftly and safely to health centers in the location, thereby decreasing the time of travel, as well as raising the individual's opportunity of living. War would certainly be significantly weak, as airpower would certainly be non-existent, the searching of opponent activities would not be feasible, and all would be battled on the ground, taking some time, resources, as well as lives.

We would certainly have never ever been to the moon either. Aeronautics led straight to the advancement of space rockets, along which brought us satellites that provides television, satellite radio, mobile messaging, navigating systems in cars as well as on phones, modern-day exact maps, and info and understanding concerning our world. Our economic climate would be considerably slower, as products could not be relocated as swiftly as well as perishable products would not have the ability to make the long trip by land without spoiling, or without huge amounts of equipment keeping them cool. Movies would certainly be bland, as airborne shots would certainly be non-existent. Ultimately, the appealing feeling as well as pleasure of air trips would just be experienced by only the birds, then the imagined trip would just remain at that, a desire, failed to remember by the early pioneers, as well as overlooked by society.

The plane is without an uncertainty the most prominent invention of the 20th century, just because it diminished the globe. It has actually linked nations that would certainly have never been connected or else, and shown us a brand-new, undetected and spectacular view of our planet. The airplane has actually come a long method because 1903, as well as still has a way to go, however, nothing comes close to the utility it brings to our quick-paced and modern-day world, and also nothing will in the near future.

Aeronautics is among the main motorists behind globalization, driving the development of the modern-day world. A network of airlines, airports as well as air web traffic administration companies link the major cities and also small areas of the globe 24-hour a day with increasingly innovative aircraft. Air travel sustains 65.5 million tasks worldwide and makes it possible for $2.7 trillion in worldwide GDR.

It permits people to have journeyed to never-been countries, to kick back on tropical beaches, to develop business connections and to check out family and friends. As our international economy grows always, aviation is the aspect that brings people together. ATAG's deal with the social and economic advantages of aviation united a globe of realities and numbers to give policymakers and also the market the essential international view of how our flight develops tasks and drives economic growth.

In October 2018, ATAG published the latest edition of its front runner report, Aeronautics: Benefits beyond Boundaries, which checks out the numerous ways in which aeronautics adds to the economy, jobs, the lives of countless individuals worldwide and also just how it contributes to lasting advancement. "It remarkably consider the extent of the aviation sector and also our duty in the world," states Michael Gill, Executive Supervisor of ATAG. When you realize that aviation was to be a country, would certainly be the 20th largest economy on the planet, supporting 65.5 million employees as well as almost three trillion bucks in economic influence, you really see the scale of air transport.

Knowing the theory behind the way a plane flies is going to open you up to the reality and would remove the aerophobia from your mind. Many still think the plane flies with some supernatural or voodoo stuff.

Over 42,000 aircraft take flight in the U.S. daily, with 5,000 in the sky at any provided time whether day or night, according to the Federal Air Travel Management. Coordinating that many arrivals, departures and also flights without crashes calls for skillful preparation, especially when it involves just how high airplanes fly.

It ends up that there's a specific altitude various aircraft should stick to while flying because of a couple of elements like the build of an airplane, the range to your location, the type of engine they have, the stamina of the winds and also the weight of the airplane.

One thing is that airplanes travel above the clouds is so they can fly quickly. The greater aircraft climb, the thinner the air becomes, and the more efficiently they can fly as a result of much less resistance in the ambience, according to Ryan Jorgenson, an air travel information analyst.

"With these bigger jets, when they take off from airports, their very first work is basically to venture out as well as obtain as high as possible as quickly as feasible," states Adam Beckman, a speaker for aviation studies at Ohio State College.

Industrial airplane generally fly between 31,000 to 38,000 feet—that's around 5.9 to 7.2 miles-- high till typically reaching their cruising elevations in the very first 10 minutes of a trip, according to Beckman.

Airplanes can fly much greater than this altitude, however that can be faced with safety and security issues. Flying higher implies it would take a longer time to return to a risk-free elevation in case of an emergency, like rapid decompression, Beckman says. It likewise isn't one of the most reliable uses of fuel to fly that high in the first place, he states, given that aircraft can fly at a reduced elevation with the assistance of the wind.

An additional reason that planes do not fly higher is because of the weight of the airplane. "The more it considers, the tougher it is to get to a certain elevation," states Jorgenson.

And the weight of the aircraft changes as the aircraft climbs higher right into the sky. "Jet fuel evaluates about 6.7 extra pounds per gallon, so the more that you burn as you're flying, you would really wind up losing a lot of gas weight," Jorgenson states. This, integrated with the thinner environment at this height, develops much less resistance.

The instructions of the wind is also a vital factor. If I'm flying to Europe from Philly, it's going to take me less time to go over there than returning. Frequently you will find that you will fly at higher altitudes when the winds are at your back.

The airplane's possible speed, additionally enhances the greater it goes. "Ten thousand feet as well as above, you can go gracefully to a much greater speed," says Dr. Thomas Carney, Teacher of Aeronautics & Transport Innovation at Purdue College. This likewise describes why you feel the airplane decreases during touchdown.

Why don't personal aircraft or helicopters fly at the very same elevation?

So why is it that tiny personal planes don't fly as high? For the most part, these planes use a piston-powered engine, which runs in a similar way to the engine in your car and with power that only allows for shorter flights, according to the National Service Aviation Association. This sort of engine stops these smaller aircraft from getting to the exact same elevations as a commercial airplane.

"The airplane that the ordinary individual can rent out and fly, those tend to remain normally below 15,000 feet that's simply a restriction on what the plane can do," Beckman states.

Pilots likewise refrain from flying these kinds of airplanes at higher heights due to prospective health risks like hypoxia, which is when tissues do not get enough oxygen, according to the National Institutes of Wellness. That absence of oxygen can take place at higher altitudes due to a decrease in oxygen pressure, according to the FAA. As the plane ascends, the degree of oxygen declines, which can trigger quick decompression for an aircraft that is not pressurized similarly as a commercial plane.

What about helicopters? Choppers are primarily made to fly close ranges and also typically fly much lower than airplanes, normally at under 10,000 feet. They are additionally not able to rise to the very same elevation an airplane can because rather than wings, helicopters have rotating blades.

So just how does the height compare to challenges overhead? Do birds ever obstruct?

Birds are most likely to block airplanes at lower elevations, and can provide issues during taking off and also landing. The extreme case of that would certainly be the United StatesAirways aircraft that arrived on the Hudson, yet that's not regular, Jorgenson claims.

But when aircraft get to normal traveling altitude, experts say birds are no more a hazard. So once the seat belt signs goes off, you can kick back and also take pleasure in the trip.

Benefits of flying over other transit methods

Let's face it, it has actually been a harsh year for flights. Beforehand, bad weather delayed hundreds of trips and left millions of vacationers stranded across the globe. But, I'm right here to inform you that we need to press those thoughts apart and proceed using air travel whenever necessary. Right here are a good number of reasons why flying is still the most effective way to travel.

It's Safe!

The old saying that flying is the best way to take a trip still applies today-- the recent track record of the airline sector notwithstanding, daily, there are more than 93,000 set up commercial airplane trips throughout the globe, and yet we can go weeks, months and years without any accident happening. When you criticize the numbers, the chances of you being onboard an aircraft that crashes are infinitesimally little. Actually, you are more probable to be struck by lightning than to be in an aircraft collision. But must your trip really drop, you're additionally most likely to still make it through.

Flight Prices Are Surprisingly Cost-Effective

It might not look like it yet when changed for inflation, airline company's ticket prices are really near an all-time low rate. As a matter of fact, they have been decreasing continuously for three decades, enabling even more of us to fly than ever. More numbered competitors, much more reliable airplanes, and also the capacity to purchase tickets for flights online have all contributed to this improvement. We are privileged to live in a period when the expense of flying is still cost-effective-- fairly talking.

It Is Still the Fastest Way to Get Anywhere

If you only have a limited number of days to travel, and also you truly wish to spend top quality time at your location, after that flying is still your best choice. If you're flying locally, possibilities are you can locate a trip that will bring you to your location early in the day, permitting you to start your holiday as soon as you arrive. If you choose to drive, you can spend days in the auto before you also reach that area, considerably minimizing the amount of time that you can spend there. And at the end of your journey, when you're ready to go home, a flight can get you there in a matter of a few hours, while encountering a return trip by auto can seem uncomfortable.

It Is the Only Way To Get To Some Places

Intend to go to Paris? Have imagined relaxing on a coastline in Tahiti? Then flying actually is the only option you have. The days of taking a slow-moving boat to Europe or anywhere else worldwide are long gone. For worldwide tourists, flying opens up nearly an unrestricted variety of opportunities, allowing us to go to remote lands, experience one-of-a-kind locations, as well as discover our earth to the maximum. Most of those places just would not be a choice for most of us without contemporary flight, and if you like immersing yourself in international cultures, then the plane is actually and figuratively your car to the world.

Inflight Home entertainment

Modern aircraft are frequently geared up with modern amusement systems that put an option of films, television shows, music, as well as games right at our fingertips. This can aid time to pass quicker while on a trip, and permit us to unwind a lot more at the same time. However, even if your airplane doesn't have an integrated home entertainment system, possibilities are you brought one with you. The majority of travelers currently come geared up with smartphones as well as tablet computers, which can fill the entertainment gap nicely.

You Can Be Effective

Bring a laptop computer with you when traveling, plus having some spare time aboard the airplane while on trip, can offer you the opportunity to be much more efficient than if you were driving to your location. If you have a longer trip, it can be the best time to take out the computer and also get some job done, and even simply back-up images from your trip. Many aircraft on domestic routes now use inflight Web also, allowing you to catch up on e-mails or check-in with family and friends back at home. Those exact same net services are coming quickly to International flights also, absolutely opening the chances to be effective while in the air.

The Sense of Community

Traveling, specifically in cheap airfare, can develop a sense of togetherness among travelers. There is commonly a feeling that everybody on the aircraft is taking a trip with each other, even if just for a brief time. This can consequently tear down obstacles and produce excellent discussions between passengers. I've found that people are generally very thrilled concerning the journey they are taking on, and they usually intend to share that exhilaration with others. On more than one event, I have had an intriguing and also fun discussion with a person that I was seated next to, which helped the trip to pass quickly. Sure, you'll periodically sit next to someone who does not seem like talking or worse yet, is a total stranger, yet usually, the sense of camaraderie that is felt in between passengers can produce a quick in-air relationship that makes the trip more satisfying.

You Can Rest!

If you're one of those fortunate guests that can doze off on an aircraft, that's sweet because flying offers you an opportunity to catch up on your rest, and reach your location relaxed, as well as all set to go. A fast nap can assist in reducing the flight-time too, as well as leave you revitalized for whatever journeys await. As somebody who isn't able to conveniently sleep on a plane, I am constantly envious of those who can.

Great Views

If you're really lucky to get a window seat, you are frequently dealt with to some birds, the horizon and wonderful sights just out the window. There is nothing quite like rising over the countryside while lakes, rivers, hills, as well as other stunning landscapes, pass underneath. Even at night, when darkness shrouds the skies, it is fun to watch out and also see the islands of light that spread across the globe visioned below you. Certainly, you can get good views from various other types of transport also, yet there is absolutely nothing that compares to the bird's eyesight you obtain from a plane.

Did I discuss that its safe?

Yes, we previously resolved this, yet it is an essential thing that I believed it deserves reiterating. It has actually been said that flying is statistically the safest way to take a trip. Exactly how secure is it? How's this for a fact? The chances of you boarding a trip that will be in a fatal accident are one in 7 million. That converts to suggesting that even if you flew daily through your entire life, you would certainly need to fly for nineteen thousand years prior to experiencing a deadly crash. That's a lot of regular leaflet miles.

All these and more benefits point to how safe flying in planes can be, aviation agencies in all parts of the world only record a few crashes per year. In fact, traveling in planes is much safer than traveling by road according to statistics.

Worry of flying or Aerophobia is a condition that can cause significant effects both physically and also emotionally to any person. This is among one of the most common phobias individuals experience. Being terrified to board an aircraft is not a simple problem. For the most part, this concern is an outcome of hidden problems that need to be treated. If you have Aerophobia, here are some things you need to understand exactly how to conquer the anxiety of flying.

Discover the Signs and symptoms

This concern can show up in numerous means. To discover the best therapy for your problem, you have to recognize the typical symptoms you may really feel when experiencing an anxiety strike due to the item of your worry. The symptoms you will experience might differ. Occasionally you will certainly experience a sign you did not experience from your previous episode.

An anxiety assault that stems from fear might have compliance with symptoms.

- Stomachache or that butterfly feeling in your belly.

- Headache

- Lightheadedness

- Nausea or vomiting

- Sweaty hands

- Difficulty breathing

- Uneasiness

An episode can happen anytime as well as anywhere especially if direct exposure to the things of anxiety impends. Occasionally, individuals also experience a panic attack just by thinking of their anxieties.

Now tackle the fear

There are many suggestions concerning exactly how to conquer flight anxieties. A few of these tips are to take sedatives before your flight and beverage relaxing beverages like champagne during the trip. While these approaches may seek to eliminate your worries, these are simply short-lived approaches of doing away with your phobia. You will be still hesitant of flying.

If you never wish to experience a panic attack as a result of your anxiety once more, you have to find a therapy that will certainly help you completely remove your fear. There are numerous options you can take to sway this problem.

Medicine treatment works best with psychotherapy but these therapies work on their own. With medication therapy, your medical professional would professionally recommend drugs that can help decrease the frequency of your strikes. Psychiatric therapy works best for anxieties as in this sort of treatment, you are presented with several things you can and in fact do things, to not be frightened anymore. Exposure treatment is a technique utilized to aid you in overcoming your fear. In this approach, you will progressively be exposed to your fear in regulated situations until you are not terrified any longer. You will certainly discover just how to get over the worry of flying by enduring the item of your phobia.

Traveling by air is just one of the most convenient means to take a trip. Do not miss the possibility to experience this convenience just because you are terrified of it. There is absolutely nothing to be scared of. Face your fear and you will certainly see what you have actually been missing out on for a long period of time.

When you have an anxiety of flying or flying anxiousness, it can be difficult, however your life doesn't need to be bereft to doing this if you recognize exactly how to get going in getting rid of worry of flying. The method you begin to employ in combating your worry of flight can make all the difference in your success, so it is very important to recognize that there are several procedures to get you to begin that which would be best for you and that which you'll be able to utilize well.

Just how much Do You Know?

You require to learn more about aircraft, it has been mentioned in the earlier chapters above though. Knowing the personnel that handle them, that repair them and the people who fly them in an initiative to getting rid of fear of flying.

Currently, this does not include reading stats regarding exactly how risk-free it is to fly as well as it does not indicate that you require to review as well as over in your head the not likely opportunity that the airplane will crash.

You do, nevertheless, need to know that there are people who work themselves extremely hard to make sure that your aircraft will certainly land you safely and comfortably to your destination and also the only means to comprehend this is to "Trust" individuals that are accountable for keeping you safe.

For example, do you understand how many evaluations an airplane must go to have the ability to fly at any moment? Each time an airplane lands, there is a thorough evaluation of the engines, the wings, and all the parts of a plane to make sure that everything remains in proper functioning order. Plus, do you know who is flying your plane? You should. A lot of your pilots have households, families, wives, children, etc., so they are going to appreciate getting to and from their locations equally as much as you do which will certainly make a difference in your heart exactly how risk-free you are.

Understanding the functions of the flying process will certainly aid you to really feel a little safer and also a little extra safe and secure concerning flying as well as might even assist to take you toward overcoming the worry of flying.

Assistance from Family Members or Buddies

It's hard to be worried of something, and also for many people, the idea of having an incapacitating concern can be incomprehensible. This implies, even if you are making efforts to battle your flight anxiety and do not have a solid support system who recognizes the way that you are feeling, you could refrain in addition to your abilities. So, the next thing you need to do is either talk to your family and friends that recognize just how negative your situation is that you are going to begin fighting your anxieties and ask for help, or sign up with a support group with others who are similar to you.

Usually, when you pick to sign up with a support system of people that are in the very same scenario as you are, you could locate that you have the ability to have even more opportunities to be understood in your pursuit of getting rid of issues with regards to flying.

Frequently, getting going in the battle your fear to fly can be the hardest part of the whole process, however, if you understand the ideal actions to take and have someone to provide you the periodic nudge, you could locate that you're flying fearlessly along in a snap. You can do it. You just require to know how to get going in overcoming your concern about flying.

If you have a phobia of flying you would certainly not realize the enjoyment that your other travelers have when they are airborne the airplane and flying a thousand feet in the air. Whereas as for you, you were so stressed out on your seat. The concept of flying is already sufficient to make you sweat excessively and also begin to flutter. You have this type of sensation due to the fact that your illogical fear is your resource of information. There are a number of individuals who are hooked with flying that they want to do it daily if they are offered the opportunity. In fact, they enjoy watching flicks about flying and also airplane. Some would go also for the purpose of taking images of various airplanes, wishing they are seated on the pilot's seat maneuvering it via the air. They try to find means to satisfy their impulse to fly. And also when they miss out on a chance; they get too upset for letting it go.

However, for individuals that are dealing with the anxiety of flying just like you, this is all a piece of crap! You would most definitely hate them if they welcome you for a flight or simply view a stirring aircraft with them. You negate them in everything they do that is related to flying. But having anxiety about flying will do no good to you. If you do not know just how to get over concern of flying, you will be embedded in your residence being all to yourself while the rest are having fun to their preferred destination throughout the nation. Or the worse, no discounts for you and also you will continue to be in the most affordable setting simply because you always make reasons for service journeys abroad; as well as the reason for thatyou are afraid to fly.

On the other hand, why not attempt to convert your anxiety right into becoming your passion? Although this may seem too impossible however it will surely help you a whole lot. Undertaking a treatment for your anxiousness will be your initial step. As you go through the procedure, you will gradually get comfortable with the concept of keeping up in the air. This is the preliminary step in eliminating all your negative impacts about airplanes. However, you likewise have to be cooperative when you make a decision to take place a therapy. There has to be a handful of decision and a basket of persistence within you. Without any of these needs, you can never ever conquer anxiety of flying. And every little thing will be pointless.

As soon as you have actually gradually grasped the charm (so to speak) of flying, you can now carry on to the following step which is learning to love it. Usually, prior to you start getting fascinated with something, you need to be experienced about it. It helps if you experience a number of resource materials that discuss flying and also aircraft. There are numerous publications, magazines, DVDs and also various other references that will persuade you that flying is a good thing to get hooked with. Also throughout the internet, there are plenty of sites that will open your eyes to the exciting world of flying.

Discovering to love your concern is a good way of diverting your bad thoughts into good ones. Do not allow your anxiety to eat you. But get rid of the fear of flying rather! Be familiar with these engines flying, scrutinize those soaring jet planes. By immersing yourself bit by bit right into these things, you will eventually understand that you are currently a plane fanatic.

Are you like the one in five that are in sheer fear as you're resting on an airplane hurtling down the path in the direction of a nearly particular fatality? Is your heart auto racing and your lungs breathing hard till the last before you take off? Having a fear of flying isn't nice however it's generally extremely simple to get over anxiety of flying! I understand I made use of these to beat flying anxiety and I developed the ability to beat it and so can you. You just have to know where to start.

Why should you overcome anxiety of flying? Not treating it is possibly making life very frustrating for you. You either cannot or won't fly overseas or to one closeby state for a holiday. You most likely have actually seen far away from loved ones as well as friends in a long period of time unless you don't feel related to them, and also your white-collar opportunities may be experiencing setbacks if you do not take a trip or take a trip as soon as you should.

Did you recognize that a lot of the moment, your anxiety is based on unreasonable ideas instead of factual details? Many times, when you remain in a plane, your mind is translating it as an unsafe circumstance as well as sending out all the wrong signals to your body. These signals motivate the fight or flight reaction, which subsequently boosts your breathing rate and also triggers a number of various other symptoms such as prickling in the lips, arms, and legs. Your chest might also really feel strangely restricted, and you might find that far-fetched, but you'll nearly look like you are choking.

At the time, it might even seem like you are having a heart attack because of your mind's incorrect signals. Naturally, if you actually do think you are having genuine clinical worries, you should look for clinical help. Many times, though it's just your body reacting to the mind's perceived hazard of threat. When you learn just how to readjust your mind to recognize that it is actually in a secure environment, you will then see your worry of flying go away.

The worry of flying causes so much anxiousness that people have not taken air travel for decades. Some people travel by air after taking some anti-anxiety drugs. Nonetheless individuals experiencing severe fear of flying stress and anxiety have actually made airplanes terminate the departure. Nevertheless, if your work or service requires you to travel overseas, after that you have extremely little alternative other than searching for services to conquer the fear of flying.

Here are some useful suggestions:

1) The primary step to eliminate this issue is to understand what element of flying triggers panic and anxiousness assaults. Lack of motion and also space could be an aspect or fear of being 33,000 feet above the ground could be the triggering factor, the concern of a crash or a terrorist assault might be the

trigger or maybe because of the mechanical sound and also turbulence or it could even be due to absence of control. As soon as you have the ability to recognize the reason, then it will be much easier to find a remedy to conquer worry of flying as well as stress and anxiety strikes.

2) One more vital element is education and learning. You wouldn't be surprised to know that situations of a vehicle crash are much more than an air accident as it has been mentioned earlier. Airplanes are developed with very high degrees of precision, accuracy, and also integrity. So recognizing even more concerning air safety, aircraft reliability, history of mishaps, etc. can really help you to arm yourself to overcome the fear of flying and anxiety assaults.

3) Taking support from others as well as a lot of discussion forums online can help to regulate this issue. Be familiar with the experience and also approaches used by others that have actually efficiently conquered anxiety of flying.

4) Use relaxation techniques to bring calmness to your mind and body. This fear is such that individuals obtain an anxiety attack also when they think about taking a trip to the flight terminal. Slowly work in the direction of getting rid of the difficulty of flight terminal traveling. Then slowly plan for taking a short trip with the help of friends and also family members. When you begin getting used to overcoming the fear of flying & anxiousness strikes, it might not be long prior to you passing by the air like a bird.

SECRETS TO STOP FEARING FLYING

The anxiety of flying is extremely a complex stress and anxiety problem and substantially affects a great deal of people. Nonetheless, despite its widespread spread over millions of people, there are various ways on how to manage it.

It is frequently called aerophobia or aviophobia that is activated by a great deal of aspects as well as not simply the concept of flying.

Individuals cannot manage their emotions &responses whenever they are airborne in the plane or even simply hearing stories about flying. Though, this has provided restrictions in all locations of their life, especially in their occupation.

The idea of keeping up airborne inside an aircraft can already make them really ill. They can't stand the sensation that they are hundreds of feet above the ground. This result in different reactions such as drinking frequently, extreme sweat, upset, trouble in breathing & sometimes vomiting. Sometimes it can straight away bring about one more fear, which is the worry of covered location or claustrophobia. The individual can feel muscular tissue tension, palpitations and also indigestion. Anxieties, despite what type they are, can indeed make complex an individual's health and wellness. If not provided with the correct medication, after that this will most definitely make him terribly sick.

If you are be struggling with these sorts of fears, you seriously need to take care of them as early as feasible.

Discovering just how to conquer the fear of flying can be easy yet it is the application of what you have learned is rather difficult. When you are beginning to feel the signs and symptoms, this is the moment that you require to master what you need to do. You cannot anticipate someone can comprehend and also quickly assist you when you remain in this situation. Hence, it is best to discover just how to handle on your own during emergency situations.

However, based on research study, the worry of flying does not just stem from the suggestion of flying alone. It is essentially from terrible experiences in the past that keep returning in your thoughts. A concrete example of this is when you simply showed up from your trip as well as when you are on your way home you are caught in a vehicle crash that leads you to be in critical condition for a couple of weeks. You cannot simply get rid of the accident in your head that whenever you ride the plane you can quickly remember what had actually occurred to you a couple of years back. Hence, you associate your flying right into a car or truck accident.

This may appear really complicated to comprehend however gathering adequate information regarding your condition can help you find out how to conquer the anxiety of flying. There are various interesting sources that you can collect about the worry of flying. As you happen with your research you can fully understand why your anxiety all of a sudden assault you and how to effectively handle it.

Psychologists and therapists would certainly encourage that it is all up to the person's willpower that he can fully handle all his fears. It requires teamwork as well as a great deal of persistence prior to he can effectively ride the aircraft with fun and excitement.

Thus, if you do not intend to miss fifty percent of your life due to your anxiety of flying, after that better begin your self-medication currently!

To soar means more than simply to fly; it's the method to rise swiftly, to sense the wind slipping beneath you as you trip it higher, higher, and higher. Flying is simply moving through the air.

Many people love journeying and seeing new places, however, there's one part of the tour that isn't so fun: flying. For some, flying is clearly a hassle, thanks to seemingly costly fares, flight delays, and lost luggage. But for other tourists, flying is more than inconvenient; it's terrifying. Fear of flying can be brought about by a number of factors, along with claustrophobia or worry of heights. Many anxious flyers experience irrational tension that their aircraft will malfunction and crash, irrespective of how many times they hear the data of how safe flying is compared to driving on roads. Other tourists worry about terrorist hijackings or panic at the idea that they're no longer on top of things of the aircraft that's wearing them.

No matter the reason you're fearful of flying, there are sure steps you may take to assist you to alleviate your fears. Flying is a personal decision and one which is such no one else can make for you. But for the ones who are determined now not to let this transformation affect their way of life, below are a few recommendations for overcoming your fear of flying.

For many frightened flyers, studying the fundamentals of the way airplanes work can bridge a long gap toward alleviating their anxiety. For instance, tapping into how a plane can preserve to fly even though an engine fails can help you feel much less involved approximately your plane malfunctioning.

This might look like a no-brainer, but it'swell worth mentioning:

 Avoid airplane catastrophe movies, news coverage of aircraft crashes, or other horrifying digital images. Recall that the vast majority of flights arrive safely but the problem is flights make the most news when any mishap happens. Don't let that cloud your travel experiences. In the days for your trip, it's smooth to allow the flight tension set in. If it does, combat your fear of flying with the thrilling prospect of getting to be on an aircraft, with a bunch of luck of going somewhere fun. Try to focus on the positive things, know you will do all that matters, you'll do as soon as you reach your destination.

Fear of flying is the fear, flying in an airplane, or other flying vehicles, which includes a helicopter, or a private jet (sounds nice right?). It is also cited as flying anxiety, flying phobia, flight phobia, aviophobia or aerophobia (although the final also way a worry of drafts or of clean air). Acute anxiety caused by flying may be handled with anti-anxiety medication. The condition may be treated with exposure therapy, which works higher when mixed with cognitive behavioral therapy. People with the worry of flying feel intense, chronic fear or anxiety whilst they don't forget flying, as nicely as all could be through flying. They will avoid flying in the event that they can, and the worry, tension, and avoidance cause big distress and impair their capacity to function. Take-off, horrific weather, and turbulence appear to be the most anxiety-provoking elements of flying. The maximum extreme manifestations can include panic attacks or vomiting on the mere sight or pointing out of a plane. Around 60% of humans mingle with fear of flying while having some other anxiety disorder.

Aerophobia, or the fear of flying, can be related to numerous other phobias, however, on some occasions, it seems to be on its own. The fear of flying is estimated to have an effect on as many as one in three persons on the average, even though a full-blown phobia is significantly less common. Travel delays, not unusual whilst flying at busy times, can make the fear of flying worse. Whether or no longer your fear of flying has developed right into a phobia, it may have devastating results on your general life.

Symptoms of Aerophobia:

The signs and symptoms of aerophobia, also known as aviophobia, are similar to those of any unique phobia. Physical signs and symptoms of the concern of flying may include:

- Shaking
- Sweating
- Gastrointestinal distress
- Heart palpitations
- Flushed skin
- Feeling disoriented
- Clouded thinking
- Irritating feelings

Some individuals with a fear of flying are reasonably snug at the airport, however, they start to experience these signs just before boarding the plane. Others have issues that begin as quickly as they reach the airport. Anticipatory anxiety, in which you begin experiencing the worry of flying long before a scheduled flight, is totally common. A fear of flying that isn't always due to medical worries or different phobias can be caused by a range of factors, including:

Experiencing a disturbing flight or plane crash: Watching a number of news coverage of airline screw-ups can be sufficient to cause a fear of flying. For example, a whole lot of the United States of America developed some form of worry of flying within the wake of the 9/11 attacks.

Environment:

If your mother and father suffered from a fear of flying, you could have internalized their trepidation. This is particularly not an unusual reason for agoraphobia in kids but impacts many adults as well. You might choose up the worry of flying from some other relative or friend, but parents seem to have the largest influence on phobias.

Other associated circumstances: Your aerophobia might also be rooted in a completely exclusive conflict. For example, a fear of flying that develops quickly after a job merchandising that calls for travel may be due to issues about the process itself or its effect on your everyday life. Likewise, youngsters who ought to fly often to go to divorced dad and mom now and again expand aerophobia as a coping mechanism for the trauma of the divorce or other life tragic experiences. Fortunately, the worry of flying is relatively clean to deal with, even without knowing the underlying cause.

Some common treatments include:

Individual treatment: Personal cognitive-behavioral treatment, hypnosis, and also digital reality techniques can likewise boost your anxiety of flying.

Education:

Knowing exactly how planes work, why disturbance happens, and also what various sounds and bumps indicate likewise can assist.

Exposure:

Experts agree that the first-best way to triumph over the fear of flying is controlled exposure, whether that's thru virtual truth, a flight simulation, or honestly flying.

Anxiety management strategies:

Learning a way to breathe deeply, apprehend panicked and irrational thoughts and correct them, and locating other approaches to manage such as being attentive to some good audios, taking an anti-tension medication, or reading magazines, can all help manage aerophobia.

Group classes:

Also, another solution is taking worry about the flying alleviation course. This has been mentioned earlier but it's being iterated for emphasis sake. These classes generally go on for two-three days, frequently over a weekend, and use strategies of cognitive-behavioral therapy (CBT) to deal with a big organization simultaneously. They are available in many principalities.

Most people love to travel and see new places, yet one aspect of the trip is not that fun traveling. For some, thanks to high fares, flight delays, and lost luggage, travel is literally a hassle. Yet traveling is more than uncomfortable for other travelers; it's scary.

Fear of flight could bring about some factors, which include claustrophobia or worry of heights. Many frightened flyers sense irrational tension that their plane will malfunction and crash, no matter how normally they hear the reports on how safe flying is as compared with driving. Many passengers are worried about terrorist hijacking or fear about the notion that they no longer control the aircraft wearing them.

Now remember why you're frightened of flying, there are certain steps you could take to help alleviate your fears. To fly or now not to fly is a personal decision and one that no one else could create yourself. But for those of you willing to no longer allow this alteration in your way of life, below are a few suggestions for overcoming your fear of flying.

For many frightened flyers, getting to know the fundamentals of the way airplanes work can do much towards ensuring their tension. For instance, have a brief knowledge of how a plane can retain it's flying stance even supposing an engine fails lets you reduce thinking your aircraft would malfunction.

Trying to get to know what your plane looks like, could make it look a lot less horrifying. I once heard of an anxious flyer who actually placed an image of the aircraft's cabin on her computer's desktop and by the point her flight rolled around, the photo changed into something familiar, not scary anymore now.

Choose an Aisle Seat; most airways and reserving engines let you make a seat assignment when you book your flight. Request an aisle seat, specifically if you're vulnerable to claustrophobia; you'll be less hemmed in by using different human beings, and you'll have the ability to rise up and move around the cabin more easily. This additionally makes it less difficult to keep away from looking out the window if the sky perspectives make you frightened.

Monitor Your Media Intake; this might also look like a no-brainer, but it's really worth mentioning: Avoid airplane catastrophe movies, news coverage of plane crashes, or different scary media images as stated earlier also. Remember that the big majority of flights arrive safely, but simplest the hassle of flights provides news headlines. Don't let that affect the flying experiences.

Be Optimistic; letting the flight stress to develop in the main day up to your trip is common. If this happens, combat your fear of flying with the exciting prospect of being on an aircraft, with some luck traveling somewhere nice. Try to be aware of the positive things you will do when you reach your destination. Many tense flyers are bothered by their perceived lack of management since they haven't any impact over the protection or overall performance of the plane. Try to regain a little self-management by reminding yourself of the reason you made the choice to fly and that you may decide how you respond to the experience.

As tension increases, your respiration can also get deep, aware-respiration is an instant stress reliever. Breathe slowly and deeply for a moment preferably five or ten minutes, in through your nose and out through your mouth.

Although this little bit of advice may appear pale, respiratory is arguably a great manner to vanquish tension. Dr. Wehrenberg explains that managed breathing works because "respiratory is the one element that will forestall a panic assault."

Turning at the air vents above your head, leaning back. Moreover, your eyes could also help you to not experience claustrophobic patterns.

Other calming, meditative tricks include sniffing a lavender sachet or sucking on a peppermint. Pack a magazine, a good e-book, or a puzzle to take your thoughts from what's going on.

Order a comedy on the in-flight entertainment network of your plane, or preload some of your favorite flicks to your laptop. Make sure you stock up on things that would last you through the period of your flight and that you could maintain to revel in whilst it's time to show electronic gadgets off.

Many fearful flyers turn to alcohol to calm their nerves. While this isn't really cool, have in mind that alcohol should now not be mixed with anti-anxiety medications.

Also, alcohol can contribute to dehydration, particularly within the arid environment of an aircraft. If you do deal with yourself to a cocktail, be sure to comply with topping with lots of water.

Recognize the stress is natural, and it's going to pass. When you do sense fearful of losing manipulation and succumbing to fear throughout the flight, remind yourself that even a full-on a panic attack is simply a brief affliction; you'll get through.

Develop Confidence

If you are low in self-belief, is it possible to do a stuff that you would be able to trade with? Is your self-confidence in your management?

While it could no longer seem so if you are low in self-confidence, I strongly believe that you can do matters to drive back your self-confidence. It isn't always genetic, and also you do now not have to be reliant on others to raise your self-confidence. And if you consider you aren't very competent, not very smart, no longer very attractive, etc. that may be changed.

You can become a person worthy of respect, and someone who can pursue what he wants despite the nay-saying of others.

You can do that by taking control of your life, and taking control of your self-confidence. By taking concrete actions that enhance your competence, your self-image, you could raise that self-confidence, without the help of anyone else.

And you don't want to do them all, as if it had been a select option and pick the ones that appeal to you, maybe just a few at first, and give them a try. If they work, then they aim for others. If they don't, then try others.

They are here, in a simple order:

1. *Groom yourself:* This seems like such an apparent one, but it's extremely good for your self-image. There were days once I grew to become my mood around absolutely with this one little component.

2. *Dress well:* A corollary of the first object above in case you dress nicely, you'll experience precisely, the exact yourself. You'll feel a success, become presentable and geared up to address the world. Now, dressing nicely means something special for

everyone. It doesn't always mean purchasing a $500 worth an outfit, but could even mean casual clothes that are just fine fitting and presentable.

3. *Photoshop your self-image:* Our self-image means so much to us, more than we frequently realize. We have an intellectual picture of ourselves, and it determines how assured we are in ourselves. But this image isn't constant and immutable. You can trade it. Use your mental Photoshopping skills, and work for your self-picture. If it's no longer an excellent run, alter it.

4. *Think tremendously*: One of the things I learned once I started my business, approximately two years ago, is how to replace bad minds with superb ones. How I can actually trade my mind, and via doing so make incredible things happen. With this tiny little skill, I become capable of educating and

making huge accomplishments each year. Sounds so kind of nice Peale, but this works out to my goodness.

5. *Kill poor thoughts:* Goes hand-in-hand with the above point, however, it's so vital that I made it a separate object. You must learn to be aware of your self-talk, the mind you have got about yourself and what you're doing. When I stepped up with some things in my life, occasionally my mind might begin to say, "This is too difficult. You need to stay away and just go watch TV." Well, I soon found out to understand this poor self-talk, and soon I found out a trick that changed the entirety in my life: I might imagine that a bad idea becomes a bug, and I might vigilantly be on the lookout for those bugs. When I caught one, I might stomp on it (mentally of course) and squash it. Kill it dead. Then substitute it with a powerful one.

6 *Get to know yourself:* The wisest when he goes into combat learns to understand his enemy very, very properly. You can't defeat the enemy without understanding him. And when you're trying to overcome a terrible self-image, anxiety and flight fears then replace it with self-belief, your enemy is yourself. Get to realize yourself well. Start paying attention to your thoughts. Start writing a journal fully about yourself, and then the thoughts you have regarding yourself, and analyzing why you have such bad thoughts. And then reflect on consideration on the good stuff about yourself, the things you may do nicely, the belongings you like. Start considering your barriers, and whether they're real boundaries or simply ones you've allowed to be positioned there, artificially. Dig deep inside yourself, and you'll come out (eventually) with even greater self-belief.

7. *Act superb*: More than just thinking effective, you have to put it into motion. Genuine action is an important thing to developing self-confidence. You are just what you are doing, and so in case you change what you do, you inline change what you're. Act in a tremendous way, take movement rather than telling yourself you can't, be high quality. Talk to people in a tremendous way, position energy into your movements. You'll soon start to be aware of the difference.

8. *Be kind and beneficial*: Oh, so corny. If that is too corny for you, then pass. But for the relaxation of you, realize that being kind to others, and generous with yourself is a first-rate approach to enhance your self-image. You act according in line with the Golden Rule, and also you start to be ok with yourself, and to think that you are a true Person. Believe me, it does wonders for your self-confidence.

9. *Get prepared*: It's difficult to be assured in yourself in case you don't suppose you'll do properly at something. Beat that feeling by getting ready yourself as much as possible. Think as if you're taking an exam: if you haven't studied, you won't have plenty of self-confidence in your capabilities to do nicely. But if you've been practicing your butt off you're good, and also you'll be lots extra assured. Now think about existence as your exam, and prepare yourself.

10. *Know your concepts and stay with them*: What are the principles upon which your existence is built? If you don't recognize them, you may have trouble, due to the fact your lifestyle will experience a directionless pattern. For myself, I try to keep the Golden Rule (and still fail). It's my fundamental principle, and I'm trying to live my existence in accordance with it. I even have others, but they may be basically in some way related to

this rule (the predominant exception being to "Live my Passion"). Think about your ideas you would possibly have them but possibly you haven't given them plenty of concepts. Now reflect on consideration on whether or not you really stay on these concepts, or in case you simply believe in them however doesn't act upon them.

11. *Speak slowly:* Such an easy factor, but it can have a huge difference in how others understand you and how you understand yourself. An individual in charge, with confidence, speaking slowly. It displays self-confidence. A man or woman who feels that he isn't worth listening to will talk quickly, due to the fact he doesn't want to maintain others on something which is not worth taking note of. Even in case, you don't experience the self-confidence of someone who speaks slowly, attempt doing it a few

times. It will make you experience greater assuredness.

12. *Stand tall*: I actually have a funny posture, so it will sound hypocritical for me to give this advice, however, I am aware that it works because I attempt it regularly. When I remind myself to face tall and straight, I experience higher approximately. Imagine if I can see a cord pulling the pinnacle of my head in the direction of the sky, and the relaxation of my frame straightens accordingly. Individuals who stand tall and assured are greater attractive. That's a suitable aspect any day, in my book.

13. *Increase competence*: How do you experience greater competence? By becoming extra equipped. And how do you do that? By reading and practicing. Just do small bits at a time. If you want to be an extra ready writer, for example, don't try to

tackle the whole profession of writing all at once. Just begin to write more. Journal, blog, write quick stories, perform a little freelance writing. The greater you write, the higher you'll be. Set aside 30 minutes an afternoon to write (for example), and the practice will boom your competence.

14. *Set a small purpose and achieve it:* People frequently make the error of taking pictures for the moon, and then after they fail, they get discouraged. Instead, shoot for something a good deal greater achievable. Set an aim you know you could reap, and then gain it. You'll feel excellent about that. Now set some other small aim and reap that. The more you attain small desires, the better you'll be at it, and the better you'll experience. Soon you'll be putting bigger (but nonetheless achievable) dreams and attaining the ones too.

15. *Change a small habit*: It need not be a huge one, like quitting smoking But just inculcating a few tiny habits, like writing matters down or waking up 10 minutes earlier than your usual time or consuming a glass of water when you wake up. Something small which you realize that you may do. Do it for a month. When you've finished it, you'll sense like one million bucks.

16*. Pay attention to solutions*: If you are one who complains, or pays less attention to issues, exchange your cognizance now. Focusing on solutions as an alternative to problems is one of the pleasant things you may do for your self –confidence and your career. "I'm fat and lazy!" So how can you resolve that? "But I can't inspire myself!" So how can you resolve that? "But I don't have any energy!" So what's the solution?

17. *Smile*: Another cool one. But it works. I sense instantly better once I smile, and it enables me to be kinder to others as well. A little tiny component that could have a sequence answer. Not a bad investment of your energy and time.

18. *Volunteer*: Related to the "be generous" object above, but more specific. It's the vacation season right now can you find the time to volunteer for an awesome cause, to spread a few excursion cheers, to make the lives of others higher? It'll be some of the satisfactory time you've ever spent, and an awesome side gain is that you'll sense better approximately yourself, instantly.

19. *Be thankful*: I'm a firm believer in gratitude, as all people who've been studying this blog for very long are aware of well. But I positioned it here because at the same time as being thankful for what you've got in life,

for what others have given you, is a completely humbling activity it could also be a completely high-quality and profitable activity with the intention to enhance your self-image. Read greater.

20. *Exercise*: Gosh, I appear to place this one on almost every listing. But I would have done you a great injustice if I had left this list. The exercise was one of my most empowering activities in the closing couple of years, and it has made me feel so much better approximately myself. All that's needed to be done by you is, stroll a few times for a week and you will see positive changes.

21. *Energize yourself with knowledge:* educating yourself is, in principle, one of the top-quality techniques for building self-confidence. You can do this in many approaches, however, one of the surest

approaches to empower yourself is through knowledge. This is along the identical vein as constructing competence and getting organized by becoming more knowledgeable, you'll be greater assured and you turn out to be extra informed via doing research and studying. The Internet is a brilliant tool, of course, but so are the people around you, humans who've accomplished what you want, books, magazines, and educational institutions.

22. *Do something you've been procrastinating on*: what is on your to-do list? Pick it up and do it immediately.

These tips are definitely unique and worthwhile, they'll help you overcome lack of confidence generally and even help keep confidence with regards to your trips via the airways.

Do you get high-strung, fearful, or afraid when you take into consideration traveling? Have you long ago even quit taking into consideration traveling since you know you cannot do it? Is somebody in your life disturbed with you because you "will not" travel with them? After that, you might be one of the many people dealing with Traveling Anxiousness. In fact, you might even have a full-blown phobia of travel.

Often these Traveling Stress and anxiety troubles are generalized to any form of travel. This suggests that the individual is incapable of taking a trip throughout any kind of form of transportation. For others, anxiety is extra specific. In particular, I suggest that the individual can drive a car and truck, ride a bus, or train. However, the idea of flying in a plane brings terror into their mind and body. Others can drive an automobile anywhere; however, riding as a passenger creates fear or a phobic response that stops them from going.

Below are some of the typical Travel Anxiousness or anxiety issues that people present to me:

The Concern of Traveling.

This client is someone who can make use of most other forms of travel; however, they can't hop on a plane. In the condition's lesser type, the person has an extreme worry and also needs medicine or/and alcohol to endure the distressing sensation connected with flying in an airplane. The individual might intellectually recognize that the plane will certainly get here safely. They understand the stats regarding car vs. flight security data. And in spite of this understanding, they remain incapacitated at the simple idea of flying.

The Worry of Driving/Riding over Bridges.

This customer shivers at the idea of crossing a bridge either as a chauffeur or passenger. Some people are a little better if they are the motorist. Many individuals avoid bridges to be merely staying home or driving considerably out of their method to take a detour or a smaller bridge.

The Concern of Riding in Any Type Of Automobile Unless As The Driver.

I've had a number of customers who can't ride in the back seat of a car. They report feeling entrapped as well as experience extreme anxiety signs and symptoms.

These anxieties and phobias are discovered. They aren't normally hardwired right into us at birth. Just two worries are hardwired right into us at birth. These are fear of loud noises and also anxiety of dropping (This worry of dropping is what many people experience today as fear of elevations.). These are leftover primitive "fight or trip responses" that were needed to preserve our lives when our forefathers strolled the levels and also highlands. These are afraid feedbacks were required for survival. Understanding this can help us understand and burst out of the idea patterns and behavioral responses connected with them. These actually aren't instances of pathology, but normal neurological feedback runs amok.

The signs for all of these variations of Travel Anxiousness has similarities. Customers report really feeling perturbed, anxious, stomach upset, or even nausea and also extreme worry. The discomfort from these signs frequently brings about avoidance. Individuals do not go places or do things that they may otherwise take pleasure in doing. Their lifestyle reduces. Additionally, they really feel adverse about themselves, and also the downhill spiral worsens and even worse.

Sadly, this problem becomes worse over time. It doesn't simply go away on its own. It's important to understand that when we accommodate an anxiousness, we enhance it. Let me place it in one more way. When we stay clear of the circumstance that causes the anxiousness, we take the stress and anxiety also worse next time, as well as the time after that, as well as the time afterward. It just worsens and also worse and also worse. Encountering your fears is an excessively simplified solution. However, it's right on target. However, best of luck keeping that. Avoidance works so well that extremely few individuals will simply press through the anxiety.

So just how do you conquer the problem? It's all about the means you think as well as reply to the anxiousness. Remember, the 'stress and anxiety' is your neurology responding to a stimulus. It's absolutely nothing more than that. You believe primarily in images, or speaking in your head. Begin by thinking about those moments you were totally positive. Not kicked back, yet absolutely confident. It doesn't require to be travel-associated. Consider this numerous times and obtain the confident state anchored actually solid. After that, Feel that confidence as you watch yourself having currently finished the travel task when it's around, and your safety. That is to state, see the completion of the trip or road trip (when it's around), and also notification that you can keep the confident experiences as you do so. Do this several times. Then, see yourself take the journey from start to end, feeling the certain overall feelings right with— exercise future trips over as well as over again. Your body and mind do not know the difference between actual as well as a visualized practice session.

The majority of people report being "in" the been afraid experience when they have anxiousness. To put it simply, they are "linked" into the experience. They persevere in their own eyes as if they were experiencing it currently. The other choice is to view on your own in the experience. This is likewise called a "dissociative" state. It is essentially impossible to have stress and anxiety when we see ourselves from afar, nonetheless much that may be. This is a valuable tool. If you have experienced a dissociative disorder in the past, it may be best to consult your medical professional prior to using this. Most of us will not have a problem with it.

This is much easier than you believe in conquering. It's also simpler when you do it with a knowledgeable clinician trained to aid you to get rid of such an issue. Most people assume it will certainly take a long time to overcome. It can take a while, yet only if you would certainly like it to. Or, you can open your mind to the opportunity that it could take place a lot more rapidly.

I constantly ask my customers, "How much time do you think it will certainly take you to conquer this trouble." The factor for this is that I need to know my customer's very own suggestions regarding how long it will certainly take. Typically, I need to honor their belief system and also job within it prior to I can alter it. Understanding a little concerning the other person's "Model of the World" can access me to various degrees of understanding of the problem. If I don't do this, we will not reach where we want to obtain as quickly as we wish to arrive. It's as straightforward as that.

Understanding my client's idea system, nonetheless, can likewise allow me to use the pointer that we transform it. Beliefs aren't repaired and long-term. We have all changed belief systems various times in our lifetimes.

Consider altering your beliefs or "Model of the Globe" also to make change happen extra swiftly. Once more, beliefs and also models aren't fixed. They were developed, and also brand-new ones can equally as easily change them.

Learning to secure a clever state, and purposefully dissociate to develop self-confidence and also effectively rehearse will certainly get you going quicker than you ever before fantasized feasible. Seeing points from a brand-new perspective is powerful and also life-altering.

I believed I would certainly talk about my experience with EFT touching and exactly how it is assisting me with my anxiety of flying. The idea, in fact, came to me today, while I got on an airplane! To start off, I would not actually call what I had an "anxiety" as it was much less extreme. It was a sort of nervousness and also discomfort that would begin as soon as I started packing my travel suitcase, and also just finish when the plane's wheels touched the ground.

Those that are familiar with EFT know that we normally rate these types of fears on a scale of 1 to 10. In my instance, I would certainly claim that my fear was between four and a 5. It would sometimes increase to a seven or even eight during the disturbance. I established to get over this anxiety completely. Not only that, but I wish to reach a point where I will, in fact, take pleasure in flying, which is not impossible cause many individuals do appreciate it.

When I first started using EFT to my concern of flying, I would tap while stating, "Despite the fact that I'm afraid of flying, I deeply as well as completely approve myself." Nonetheless, after finding out more about EFT, I realized that this setup declaration was way too broad.

I started being much more details afterward. I began touching on:

"The discomfort while packing."

"The uneasiness while going to the airport terminal (and also in the flight terminal)."

"The anxiousness while the aircraft is removing. What happens if something goes wrong?".

"The anxiousness while touchdown ...

AND SO ON".

You get the point.

After doing these tappings, I did fly a couple of times, and I did really feel extra comfy. I really felt entirely OK at the airport terminal as well as far better throughout the flight. Yet some anxiety was still there.

While considering it throughout one of my trips, I understood that this anxiety was because of some horrible photos that involve my mind regarding what might occur to the plane. Some of these pictures originate from movies I've seen in the past with scenes of aircraft crashing and such. They would come to my mind uncontrollably, and also, I was subconsciously pressing them away. But they were still returning and creating me this distress. So I figured I would describe, thoroughly, what I would certainly be afraid would certainly happen while tapping on it. As an example:

"Although I'm terrified that the engines would unexpectedly stop working and etc. (ill extra you the information). I entirely approve of myself".

An additional idea concerned me that being completely comfy on the plane is not a good idea!! (Which is certainly incorrect!) So I touched:

"Also assumed being comfortable as well as satisfied on a plane is crazy, trigger you never recognize what might occur, I accept myself and also believe that I am shielded (by God)."

So I did that and also, fortunately, the images stopped coming. Or, they would come, but they would certainly be less clear and a lot less frightening. I presume a little bit much more touching would finish the work.

CLAUSTROPHOBIA WHILE FLYING

Claustrophobia impacts tens of thousands of individuals in the UK alone. It can cause many troubles within your life, particularly when it involves flying. With this in mind, and our focus on highlighting Mental Health and wellness as well as Travel, we believed it would be interesting to discover this and talk with individuals it impacts each day.

What is Claustrophobia?

Claustrophobia is the fear of being confined or shut in a tiny space and also not being able to get out. Sufferers are commonly looking for the nearby departure and will certainly often avoid busy and also crowded areas. This sensation can expand from previous experience as well as can impact individuals' lives daily for several years. Sufferers can experience claustrophobia in work areas, little areas and also crowds and commonly these feelings are increased when on an aircraft.

Having a worry of flying as well as having claustrophobia are two various points which are often confused. A fear of flying is being terrified of the aircraft crashing resulting in injury or fatality. A claustrophobe isn't always worried about this-- they are extra distressed that the doors will not open up at the end of the flight or the departures will be obstructed with slow-moving travelers.

Top Tips for defeating Claustrophobia in the flight terminal

If you do deal with claustrophobia and also are planning a trip, here are a few of our suggestions on how to make the trip a little bit a lot more comfortable!

Visit your General Practitioner:

Once you've reserved your trips, it might be a great suggestion to book in with your medical professional to review your issues.

They may have the ability to recommend an over the counter help such as Calms to help in reducing your anxiousness, or perhaps even something prescription if your claustrophobia is especially bad.

Research your course and also airline: Flying somewhere long haul? Try and choose a straight flight and also avoid stops as well as modifications. This will certainly minimize the quantity of time you require to get off as well as re-alight a plane for in one trip. Researching your airline will likewise imply you'll know if you can pre-book seats as well as how much they remain in advancement. This is an excellent way to ensure you can rest with individuals you intend to and be close to departures if you prefer. You might even obtain additional legroom!

Reserve a lounge:

Examine the airport terminal you are flying from and also see if you can reserve some time in a lounge beforehand. These are generally much calmer and quieter areas which aren't so jampacked.

Top priority Boarding:

This can generally be added when you get your tickets online or on the phone. It is typically really inexpensive and makes sure that you can be among the first to board the aircraft. This provides you a long time to get cleared up without being jostled in the aisle.

FastTrack Security:

Supplied at numerous airports for a small charge and also can additionally become part of auto parking bundles, so it would certainly be worth signing in development. You can schedule this from just £ 3 in some flight terminals, so it actually can be worth the tiny price!

On the plane:

Make sure to pack a lot of distractions! Points like your favorite snacks, a book or even downloading and install a few movies or TV box sets to your phone or tablet computer are good ways to maintain your mind off the truth you're on an airplane.!

Claustrophobia typically is available in collaboration with another anxiety-- the concern of the unknown. Unless you take a trip routinely, flying can be a frightening idea as it's an unfamiliar environment. Whilst some businessmen and also women can get here for a trip an hr prior to they are due to take off as well as feel unwinded, various other passengers may appear three hrs before their flight taking off and also really feeling stressed.

You define the cycle of panic so well right here, Donna. What typically keeps panic in play is the fear of having another assault, in addition to various other, outer problems, like worry of shame or worry of not having the ability to function. In your instance, as you insightfully recognize, it is not flying that stresses you however the concern of panicking when you fly.

It's wonderful that you're in the aviation occupation since that forces you to confront these worries. Preventing the circumstances, you fear can enhance the feeling of panic. For instance, if you avoided flying as a method to avoid anxiety attack, the evasion would eliminate the stress and anxiety and also you would momentarily really feel far better. Of course, this would urge you to continue staying clear of flying. This cycle in fact magnifies anxiousness, and also can also convince you that an anxiety attack is unavoidable whenever you fly.

So to begin with, I congratulate you for remaining to fly although it is occasionally frightening; maintain that up! Below are some extra approaches to help you lower the risk of another anxiety attack on the trip:

While you're flying, take note of what you are engaged in when there are no elements of worry in you; you're most likely focusing on something other than your capacity to panic. Whatever we focus on comes to be enhanced in our minds, so focusing on a particular task can be rather useful.

Find out a breathing strategy to employ at the earliest indications of stress and anxiety.

There are great deals of them out there. It can end up being an important tool for you can utilize when you recognize the presence of stress and anxiety. It can likewise assist you avoid the escalation of stress and anxiety into panic.

Don't drink high levels of caffeine before or throughout the trip. High levels of caffeine can boost heartbeat and also speed your breathing, which you might misunderstand as the early indications of an anxiety attack. The really thought that you are beginning to panic can intensify the panic even more.

Make sure to include regular, moderate workout in your day-to-day regimen. It can lower the physical signs of persistent stress, which you might additionally incorrectly take very early indicators of panic.

Make sure to eat healthy foods around the moment of the trip, including healthy protein as well as fiber so that your blood glucose levels stay fairly stable. Abrupt increases in blood glucose happen whenever we eat a lot of refined, sugary foods and can trigger physical signs and symptoms like jitteriness and sweating, which can look like the starts of panic.

If you are afraid arrest and tiny locations, boarding an aircraft can be terrifying, despite exactly how made up and positive you get on land. Also, a brief trip can appear never-ending. Claustrophobia is a relatively usual anxiousness without a clear reason or sure-fire treatment. Dealing with flight-induced claustrophobia entails taking preventive actions prior to the flight and also, once you get on board, employing different devices, techniques, and actions to take control of your very own reactions, making your journey at least acceptable.

Board the airplane as late as possible. Wait at eviction till the last boarding contact us to reduce how long you have to spend on the aircraft.

Practice deep breathing as quickly as you get onto the airplane. Panicked people tend to heighten their anxiousness by taking shallow, short breaths. Shut your eyes, take a breath deeply with your nose and breathe out gradually. Repeat this kind of breathing until you feel tranquil. You may need to invest the whole flight breathing in this manner.

Maintain on your own active throughout the flight. Walk up and down the aisles whenever you're permitted. Pay attention to soothing music or an audio variation of a preferred author's publication while seated. Maintain your eyes shut or use an eye mask while in your seat as well as envision on your own in an open space. You'll be back on the ground prior to you know it.

FLY SAFELY WITH CLAUSTROPHOBIA

If you have to take flights with claustrophobia, you might fear regarding your trip. However, flying with claustrophobia need not be a calamity. Meticulously preparing your trip can assist you to maintain your fear controlled.

Picking Your Flight

Even though you may be inclined to go shopping entirely by rate, it is necessary to learn the details concerning a certain airline company, path, as well as a particular flight. It might deserve paying much more for a trip that fulfills your requirements.

Airline

At once, the traditional airline companies used a full-service experience. The budget airline companies trimmed the frills, giving confined seats, as well as a couple of solutions for a low-cost ticket. That is no longer an issue today. That airline is distinct, so meet the Line Sites to decide the latest plans.

Course

Some paths are common among service tourists, making those trips extremely crowded during the week. Others are much more popular with visitors, that usually traverse the weekend. Some flights are actually segmenting of longer paths, which means that the airplane you board may currently be crowded with those that boarded at a very early stop. Research study the path you are thinking about to discover what to anticipate.

One more consideration is whether you will certainly require to change planes. Lots of city pairs need you to fly to a central city and also board a new aircraft to your final destination.

Particular Trip

A quick internet search can give information on any type of particular flight. You can uncover exactly how crowded a flight typically is as well as its typical on-time ratio. Although there are no assurances, learning this information in advance can help you select the trip with the lowest chance of overbooking or hold-ups.

Seat

Which seat is best for you will certainly depend upon your unique demands? Lots of people with claustrophobia prefer to sit in a leave row, which provides additional legroom. Bear in mind that in order to sit in a departure row, you must be reasonably healthy and both prepared as well as able to aid in an emergency situation emptying ought to anything happen.

A window seat enables you to look outside and also take pleasure in the view. Many people really feel that this helps them to change their emphasis away from the congested aircraft.

Lounging on the aisle, helps you to fly freely. Walking supplies a break as well as can assist you handle your symptoms. It likewise gives easier access to the bathrooms, in addition to any reassuring products you have in overhead storage.

Prior to Your Flight

Before your flight, make certain to prepare with a see to your service provider, exercising coping devices, and also do your study.

Visit your physician. Numerous weeks prior to your trip, visit your doctor as well as therapist. Even if you do not generally take drugs for your fear, your physician may want to prescribe a temporary anti-anxiety drug.1 Pay cautious attention to any type of guidelines, which could consist of starting the prescription a few days ahead of time or staying clear of alcohol consumption.

Learn ways to manage symptoms. Your specialist can educate you coping approaches to use in flight. Led visualization, breathing exercises, as well as other strategies, can be used while in your seat as well as may help head off a panic attack.1.

Practice any type of brand-new techniques ahead of time, as they might take a while to feel all-natural.

Be updated on flight terminal security methods. Flight terminal security policies seem to transform on a virtually everyday basis. See the TSA website a day or 2 before your trip to ensure you recognize the latest rules regarding both carry-on as well as inspected baggage. Pack thoroughly to guarantee you are within the rules.

On Flight Day.

The day of your flight, take actions to ensure your comfort.

Allow on your own plenty of time at the flight terminal. Authorities' guidelines mention that you ought to arrive at the very least 2 hours prior to a domestic trip, as well as 3 hrs before a worldwide flight. Nevertheless, you might intend to expand that home window a bit. The stress and anxiety of a congested flight terminal and invasive safety and security screening can place you in danger for a panic attack, as well as questioning whether you will certainly make the flight will just raise your anxiety.

Be moisturized. When you are via protection, you will certainly be able to appreciate the restaurants, shops, and also features inside the safe area of the airport. Drink a lot of water and attempt to eat a small treat.

Keeping hydration and also blood sugar level is necessary for remaining tranquility.

Check in at your gateway a minimum of 30 minutes before the flight. Offering on your own a lot of time for this last step of the process will certainly aid you to stay tranquil and also concentrated.

On the Plane.

When you have actually boarded the airplane as well as you prepare to go, deal with yourself and do your ideal to handle any type of signs and symptoms you may experience.

Throughout your trip, maintain on your own sidetracked as much as possible. Bring an iPod, DVD gamer, or laptop computer or acquisition headphones and also view the in-flight flick. If you are taking a trip with a relative or buddy, engage in conversation. Slip off your footwear and also loosen up with a cushion and also covering.

If you have an anxiety attack, let you are taking a trip partner to recognize. They might be able to help chat you down.

Otherwise, concentrate on your coping approaches. Technique coping techniques. Get up as well as walk if the safety belt light is off. Go to the toilet as a well as dash cold water on your face.

Take anti-anxiety medication according to your physician's recommendations, however prevent self-medicating with alcohol. Drinking might really raise your stress and anxiety.

Ask for assistance, if you need it. Steward can manage all kind of in-flight emergencies including stress and anxiety assaults.

Although not educated specialists, they can offer different sorts of assistance. Don't be reluctant to request assistance if you require it.

MEDITATION TO RID FLYING FEAR

Reflection are a reliable means of kicking back the body and lowering anxiety, resulting in a mind that is stress complimentary. The appeal of meditation and its practice have actually assisted a lot of individuals to deal with their internal most worries and also anxiousness and also have helped them cope up with a great deal of unsettled disputes.

Anxiety of flying is a typical issue dealt with by individuals the world over. People who are afraid of flying come to be paranoid during a flight and wind up having uncomfortable feelings, elevated anxiousness, panic attacks, and even sleepless nights prior to the flight. Due to the fact that reflection is an effective mind control workout at a subconscious level, plenty of individuals resorts to it to solve their worries.

Reflection can be one of the very best ways to assist you to rid of your concern of flying or a minimum of aid you regulate it. The anxiety of flying is among the most common worries among people. The concern of flying can come to be such a problem that in some cases it can provide you sleepless evenings prior to boarding an airplane; it can provide you panic attacks to name a few stresses that can end up in your body as some type of disease.

Reflection relaxes the body and helps in reducing tension by placing your mind and body comfortable. It has assisted many that it has become a preferred method to help those with the worry of flying as well as it includes secondary benefits; it assists people manage various other worries in their lives.

The thought of Reflection occasionally stops people from eliminating their anxieties. The meditation is very easy as well as once you discover the process it can be delightful; reflection is done by several and also are taking pleasure in the advantages.

There are numerous means to find out about doing away with your flying worries; listening to CDs', reviewing online or shop-bought books, searching on-line about what people are discussing this topic. It is unlimited the readily available details.

Listening to a CD may be less complicated as it can be brought with you anywhere you go as well as you can listen while driving your automobile, in the house, at work, also before boarding an aircraft as well as during the flight.

The reflection courses will certainly assist you to eliminate your flying fears yet they will certainly likewise instruct you just how to manage various other worries you could be having; it will aid remove your anxieties concerning flying yet it will certainly serve in various other locations of concern you may have in your life.

The reflection CDs' are being offered by some airline company firms; they are starting to supply them to passengers to help them unwind aboard the plane.

They have noticed this benefit reduces both means by serving themselves as well as the more unwinded guest will certainly be more going to take a trip more often.

The airline companies have come to be extremely innovative in the types of reflection CDs' they are supplying; for taking off, for during the flight and for the touchdown.

When you learn how to get rid of your flying anxiety you will certainly relish your new improvement as well as you will certainly see a better you; you will certainly convert moments of stress and anxiety into moments of peace during your trip amongst all the other advantages that occur from discovering just how to practice meditation. You will be improved by the self-discovery and the control you are going to have in various other areas of your life.

It can be normal for an individual to have a bit of anxiety before flying on an airplane, yet those who are experiencing aviophobia manage solid symptoms of anxiety and tension which can impair their capacity to function usually. Countless individuals worldwide deal with a fear of flying. There are means to treat this trouble as well as I will certainly touch on some of them.

Firstly let's review what several of the signs and symptoms are. An individual who is suffering from aviophobia is likely to: feel nauseated, shake, tremble, vomit, really feel motion sickness, have actually an enhanced heartbeat, sweat profusely, breathing heavily, sweat as well as have stress in their muscles.

If your symptoms are severe as well as include numerous of what I just detailed after that you must make an appointment with a psychotherapist. You will certainly be asked to review when the symptoms began, just how it began as well as exactly how extreme the symptoms are. They will provide you some recommendations on how to prepare your mind for a trip.

It is common for aviophobia to happen along with various other psychological disorders. The psychotherapist will want to rule out various other troubles such as drug abuse, stress and anxiety and also clinical depression.

Many different points can create an individual to establish a fear of flying. It depends upon the person and their scenarios, essentially. Instances of what might bring about this condition is a person shedding a relative in a plane crash or severe mid-air disturbance.

All of the information about aircraft crashes on TV can make it truly hard to conquer aviophobia. So, you would want to go off the news. After the 9/11 terror strikes lots of people established anxiety of flying.

Specific natural herbs can help to soothe you down before a trip. St. John's Wort, Valerian, Passiflora Incarnata as well as Scullcap are all good at assisting you to unwind and also relaxing you down. You do not need to use all of these simultaneously but it is a great idea to experiment with them in order to see which one works best for you.

Leisure methods, such as reflection or yoga, can likewise help you to create the necessary abilities of leisure. Show yourself exactly how to control your breathing and you are one action better to being able to master your scenario on aircraft.

With every passing day, Life is becoming more and more mentally tasking, psychologically and even physically. This creates stress and anxiety levels to develop as well as certainly cause distress and also anxiety. Ultimately, it can influence your body, coming off as state of mind swings, frustrations, and even worse disorders. Meditation is a good way to fight all of that. It makes use of transporting your mind, charging it to attain mental balance. The mental balance then adds to physical equilibrium. Physical equilibrium after that causes emotional equilibrium. This proves true as reflection has located to have several health and wellness advantages. Not only does it minimize stress and anxiety, yet boosts high blood pressure as well as breathing. Reflection is typically perceived as being still to prevent interruptions.

While it is true that resting still can allow you to go into an introspective state, various other reflection methods permit you to move, so that not just is your mind in equilibrium, however likewise your body also. Movement throughout meditation involves rhythmical breathing, as well as soft, graceful actions that let your body loose. One can meditate with movement by making sluggish changes in body positions.

For instance, from a resting position, you can slowly move into a squat. Be aware of where your body components are, your feet touching the ground, your knees flexed. You can move your arms, in slow elegant waves. Relocate body parts, which really feel strained. Then you can gradually increase, moving your body in a fluctuating activity. Imagery and visions of nature can aid you to feel the activities. You can envision that you are a flower bud growing, or a pet crossing the woodland, or a bird or butterfly opening its wings and flying. Open your mind as well as permit your body to move and also get shed in the motion. You can still accord with your body even if in movement.

This permits entirety with your mind and body and detachment from the physical world. This sort of meditation can be done after basic meditation (such as resting still and listening to breathing), to make sure that not just is the mind invigorated, however, the body also.

Demographically, you are much more probable to die in a car accident than an aero-crash. If you were flying on an airplane every day, it would actually lessen your probabilities of dying. Unfortunately, rational facts seldom make a difference for phobias. From the worry of public talking to flying, our phobias are rarely rational.

For many humans, a fear of flying isn't a problem. If you hardly ever need to tour, you ought additionally never to get on an aircraft. For others, a relaxed flight is a necessity. Work tasks and family events might also make flying necessary. It can be impossible to take part without getting on an aircraft.

Can You Conquer a Fear of Flying?

While it may seem impossible, you may experience a relaxed flight. Many humans have recovered from their flying phobias through hypnotherapy. Without assistance, this phobia may be bad. A few hours on an airplane would take a number of days to travel by land. Hundreds of bucks are wasted through keeping off the airport. Rather than waste money, some human beings use equipment like hypnosis.

Over time, if not curbed, phobia of flying could hold your career, social lifestyles, and happiness. A Gallup poll indicates that 10 percent of human beings are terrified of flying. Breathing physical games and remedy may assist. The real hassle is the individual's thoughts. You believe that flying can harm you. No quantity of breathing will unexpectedly change this.

To experience a relaxed flight, many have resorted to severe measures. Some want sedatives to knock them out for the flight. Other people pretend to fly the usage of digital reality. There are self-help guides. There are phobia gurus. Out of a majority of these options, the one method that footwear the maximum promise is hypnosis.

Does Hypnosis Help a Fear of Flying?

While fear of flying can be irrational, understanding this does not stop you from feeling afraid. You might also sense jittery, nerve-racking or panicked at the concept of flying. Even when you need to fly to a holiday warm spot, your fear receives in the manner.

Hypnosis is a fantastically effective way to experience snug at the same time as flying. Like any phobia, it is rooted for your subconscious. You might also have had a traumatic experience or watched an aircraft crash. Whatever the cause, your mind is attempting to shield you. It thinks that flying is dangerous. Thus, the concern is created to warn you away from flying.

To triumph over your fear, you must deal with it. Hypnosis finds out what triggers that fear for your subconscious. Over time, a hypnotist facilitates reprogramming the mind so that you are now not afraid. Your thoughts relearn fine truths about flying. As a result, you may get away from your long-held fear.

With hypnosis, you may revel in a relaxing, calm flight. This safe remedy is absolutely natural. It instantly ends worry through methods like visualization. Before long, you are capable of flying whilst you need to. Debilitating worry no longer holds you back. Your mind relaxes absolutely. Because of this, you're capable of experiencing your flight.

As a hypnotherapist, I see quite a few humans who have precise fears and phobias. The one this is the most common is a fear of flying. Some people have continually felt anxious about flying whilst others have spent many years getting onto planes without any problem but have then advanced a worry of flying.

A lot of humans will grit their enamel and spend the complete flight and frequently days or weeks main up to it in a state of agitation and fear. Others will ask their health practitioner for medication or find their own manner of dulling their emotions. Some human beings just refuse to fly which may be limiting for both delight and paintings and can purpose friction in relationships.

Using hypnotherapy to lessen the fear of flying is a very obvious thing to do. Hypnotherapy uses hypnosis to help people make adjustments throughout their lifetime. There are many variables that are important with regard to hypnosis.

Thoughts have an effect on emotions and emotions have an effect on thoughts. In the majority of humans, feelings have an extra effect than thoughts. If something causes a robust emotion it'll have an extra effective than a logical idea. If you feel terrified, all the information that human beings inform you approximately why you shouldn't be scared won't have any effect. Your sturdy emotion overrides the logical part of your brain. Hypnosis uses a suggestion, a perception in that suggestion and then repetition of that suggestion.

So, when you have a worry of flying then you definitely are feeling hypnosis. You think about being airborne, then the worry sets in, which then makes the idea even worse which reinforces the worry. A hypnotherapist assists you to alternate those thought styles by way of decreasing the fear and permitting new thought patterns and feelings to set up themselves. If you've never felt good about flights, then you're going to be developing a new experience. If you've got flown without worry inside the beyond then you could tap into a number of your past enjoy and use that.

If you would really like to apply hypnotherapy to lessen your fear of flying then I could propose seeing a hypnotherapist for a personal consultation that is tailor-made for your unique issues.

Hypnotherapists and their classes range so it's miles critical to locate someone who you feel cushy with and who you think can help you. There are lots of ready hypnotherapists but frequently you will relate to one higher than any other or you decide upon the way in which they paintings. Find out how to pick out the nice hypnotherapist for you.

The wide variety of periods can range from 1 to 8, even though the common seems to be around three or 4. There are several reasons for this. A hypnotherapist might also choose to do greater classes because of the techniques they use or because they need to cope with the worry in greater depth. You might also need extra periods because the fear of flying is associated with other anxiety as properly and also you don't like making modifications quickly. The period of the classes can also affect the range which might be needed.

In a hypnotherapy consultation, the hypnotherapist will ask you approximately your worry. This could consist of how it influences you, how long you've had it if you understand why and while it started. You may also be requested approximately other components of your life as properly to discover if there are different factors that would be relevant.

The majority of the hypnotherapists would start the consultation by taking you into a relaxed state. This is because whilst you are comfortable your thoughts are extra open to alternate and you'll sense more comfortable. You may additionally have been given a hypnosis relaxation song to listen to before your consultation. If you find it difficult to loosen up then just permit the hypnotherapist to recognize because there are different techniques that could be used instead.

Some hypnotherapists will take you into that comfortable kingdom and then supply you suggestions for feeling comfortable while flying. They will talk to you through an exciting flying experience.

Others will use a few analysis strategies at some point in the session. They might also ask questions about your fear and your stories and then give recommendations which can be related to that.

You may also be taught a few self-hypnosis so you can use it after the session and on occasions while you're going to fly. You probably won't need to apply them for the relaxation of your life however self-hypnosis can be genuinely helpful to enhance the recommendations from the hypnotherapy periods and to offer you self-confidence for future flights. Remember suggestion, notion within the suggestion after which repetition of it. You will be following the same pattern which you used to follow whilst you notion about flying but now in a positive manner as opposed to a poor one.

The question each person desires to recognize is "what is it like being hypnotized?" One way to describe its miles that it's far a bit like daydreaming. You are aware of what's happening however your thoughts additionally drifts. It can be liked to you seeing a movie and you get totally stuck up in it. You may be aware that you're watching a movie but you also are engaged via it. People commonly say they felt relaxed. Often human beings can't explain why they sense otherwise about flying. It's just a process their thoughts have gone through and they definitely know that they do sense differently.

Another not unusual question is "will it work for me?" If you're open-minded and willing to attempt it then it's very in all likelihood that it'll work – even in case you are skeptical and don't see how it may paintings. If your subconsciousness has been making up a fear of being airborne, as I stated earlier, you have already been experiencing hypnosis. So, it's high in all likelihood that hypnosis also can assist you to remove the concern.

What's causing you worry about flying?

When moving by air is deemed to be the safest way to travel, why does your worry of flying keep to plague your journey? The business airline industry is certainly one of the maximum scrutinized styles of transportation. Just Google the facts and you may learn about a pilot's considerable training, back-up systems, maintenance, and the enterprise's excellent safety report, etc.

You can also be advised that statistically, you are much more likely to die in a riding twist of fate or in a coincidence caused inside the home. Has that reassured you sufficient to book your flight tickets?

This research information that shows that business flying is secure can offer very little comfort if you already believe that flying is dangerous. One rationalization for that is that statistics connect to the logical and rational part of your thoughts where "understanding" it's far secure can fulfill it. Feeling that flying is secure is a different thing altogether! It may be frustrating whilst that 'already-convinced-that-flying-is-safe' a buddy of yours optimistically asserts that "flying is awesome…you'll be fine!" And somehow, the ones feedback simply don't hook up with your emotions of sheer terror. If knowing this safety info doesn't reassure you, it's because your brain's tense wiring device lies below those conscious, logical colleges which can take delivery of that its miles secure. Sometimes known as the "combat or flight!" center on your brain, it's a part that is hot-wired to supply the physical stress signs and symptoms which can be normally experienced whilst you've got, rightly or wrongly, related a situation as a dangerous one. The stress signs and symptoms consist of racing coronary heart rate, shallow and fast breathing, profuse sweating, confusion, etc. These signs and symptoms are also part of the extreme tension response referred to as a panic attack.

The "fight or flight!" center is likewise strongly linked to emotions, beliefs, and memories (irrespective of whether or not the reminiscences are easily recalled or forgotten). If you have had a right away flying trauma, you could moderately expect your thoughts to protest towards any new `information" that contradicts what you already consider from the trauma that you have previously suffered. It's the indirect past "traumas' ' which could motivate the confusion to your mind, putting you on high alert while the cutting-edge situation is not `known" as a threatening one. Previous unresolved or forgotten middle threats latch onto new conditions with the aid of association until the core danger is mentioned and dealt with. Your mind is being flooded along with your beyond accumulated threat whilst looking to make the experience of the brand new apparent hazard.

What are those unresolved fearful situations which could leak into your flying enjoy and add 'fear of flying' to your chance list? Some of the more commonplace unresolved fears consist of worry of restricted spaces (claustrophobia), fear of heights (acrophobia) and worry of embarrassment induced with the aid of having a panic attack in the front of other people (social phobia). With these core problems, the original enjoy may not have directly worried flying, however, they can be related to flying in a future experience. So whilst you now have a mild feeling of tension while flying because of turbulence, for example, your mind stacks the combined anxiety and motion with past center issues which includes constrained spaces, heights or crowds. Flying turns into a new danger, despite the fact that turbulence on its own is a lesser danger. There are several unresolved fearful situations listed on this link that could be inflicting your fear of flying.

For many people, flying is a vital approach to travel. Having a severe fear of flying can damage the enjoyment of your circle of relatives' holiday. It may distract your preparation main as much as your essential work-associated meeting abroad. Deal with the middle issues which are contributing to your fear of flying and you could fly with confidence.

To overcome your fears, begin with the aid of describing them out loud to yourself, since talking about your fears will make them less difficult to triumph over. For example, you would possibly say "When I stand in small spaces, I feel anxious, but I know I'm safe." Once you've mentioned your fears, try progressively exposing yourself to them till they're now not as horrifying anymore. You might strive to stand in a closet, for example, before attempting a smaller space. However, if you get scared while you're dealing with your fears, take long, deep breaths and attempt clenching and relaxing all of the muscle tissues in your body till you feel calmer.

If you're struggling to overcome worry and anxiety about flying, try to remind yourself that other sports we perform on an everyday basis, like driving a car, are much extra dangerous. You ought to also keep in mind that turbulence, which causes a flight to experience bumpy, is entirely regular and caused by flying through low stress into excessive pressure. When you book a trip, choose an immediate flight at your destination so you must spend less time in the air. Before you fly, attempt traveling to the airport so that you can get used to being there, with the intention to help you get comfortable with the idea of flying. If you may pick out a seat for your flight, choose one over the wing, due to the fact that passengers who sit there usually revel in a smoother flight. During the flight, avoid drinking alcohol to control your worry, when you consider that it is able to definitely make you extra anxious. Instead, distract yourself with a snack or a magazine.

If you have a worry of heights, there are many methods, like rest and slow exposure, to help you conquer your anxiety. Try deep breathing or yoga and meditation to learn how to calm your body and mind. These practices can then be used when you're in a state of affairs where heights are involved. Another technique to deal with your fear is to gradually expose yourself to it. For instance, start by hiking up a huge hill and looking down over the distance you've covered. When you feel cushy doing this, push yourself a little further, like taking the elevator as much as the top floor of a hotel. Celebrate every accomplishment as you slowly conquer your fears.

Fears are healthy due to the fact it guards us against a dangerous scenario. It no longer counts if the harmful scenario is actual or imaginary, the important difficulty here is that for us it is a dangerous state of affairs.

It places us on alert and we can prepare to face the state of affairs. Start overcoming your fears to experience the existence you need to live. Learn to manipulate yourself, and eliminate it.

The points stated in this book of the title; **FLY WITH NO FEAR** with the subtitle;

STOP FLYING WITH PHOBIA! END PANIC, ANXIETY, CLAUSTROPHOBIA AND FEAR OF FLYING FOREVER! OVERCOME YOUR ANTICIPATORY ANXIETY AND DEVELOP SKILLS TO HAVE A CONFIDENT & RELAXED FLYING

Are such that should be followed so as to see changes and rid yourself off that fear completely.

This Document aims to provide precise and reliable details on this subject and the problem under discussion.

The product is marketed on the assumption that no officially approved bookkeeping or publishing house provides other available funds.

Where a legal or qualified guide is required, a person must have the right to participate in the field.

A statement of principle, which is a subcommittee of the American Bar Association, a committee of publishers and Associations and approved. A copy, reproduction, or distribution of parts of this text, in electronic or written form, is not permitted.

The recording of this Document is strictly prohibited, and any retention of this text is only with the written permission of the publisher and all Liberties authorized.

The information provided here is correct and reliable, as any lack of attention or other means resulting from the misuse or use of the procedures, procedures, or instructions contained therein is the total and absolute obligation of the user addressed.

The author is not obliged, directly or indirectly, to assume civil or civil liability for any restoration, damage, or loss resulting from the data collected here. The respective authors retain all copyrights not kept by the publisher.

The information contained herein is solely and universally available for information purposes. The data is presented without a warranty or promise of any kind.

The trademarks used are without approval, and the patent is issued without the trademark owner's permission or protection.

The logos and labels in this book are the property of the owners themselves and are not associated with this text.